beautiful buggy walks

england

by

Richard Happer

Beautiful Buggy Walks: England
Published in the UK in 2012 by
Punk Publishing Ltd, 3 The Yard, Pegasus Place, London SE11 5SD
www.punkpublishing.co.uk
www.beautifulbuggywalks.co.uk

A catalogue record of this book is available from the British Library.

ISBN 978-1-906889-53-1
10 9 8 7 6 5 4 3 2 1

To my beautiful buggy walkers – Rachel and Harry.

contents

introduction

When you're a new parent you can't wait to show your child the world. And to show the world your child... You want to bond with your new family and find an activity you can all do together. If you're a mum, you'll also want to get outside for a bit of exercise and some fresh air after weeks of restricted mobility. You probably want to keep an eye on your expenses too.

A walk is the perfect family activity – it puts smiles on faces, tones muscles, fills young lungs with fresh air and gives you a day out together amid some stunning scenery. It's more natural than going to the gym and, best of all, more often than not it's free.

But it can be harder than you might think to find an easy-rolling route for your buggy. Famous beauty spots like the Yorkshire Dales are stuffed full of stiles, and it can be frustrating to set off on a lovely wide Cornish footpath only to discover it becomes a rocky scramble half a mile around the corner.

So we wheeled several willing young volunteers along hundreds of miles of perfect paths (and dozens of dead ends) in the most picturesque corners of England. We explored secret city wanders and thrilling highland getaways. We rolled along epic coastal paths and around elegant country estates. Over hill and dale, by rivers and canals – we've done the legwork and selected 50 stunning strolls that are also easily 'buggyable'. You can roam from the cliff-tops of Perranporth on Cornwall's Atlantic shore to the remote moorland around Kielder Water in

Northumberland, taking in every stripe of English countryside in between. There truly are some unforgettable outings here.

Several walks have 'added extras' – a ferry ride, a steam train, a beach – to help keep older kids amused (forget 'soft play', head for the forest!) and your day out packed. We point out the best cafés, attractions, child-friendly pubs – and loos – along the way. We've included a selection of fascinating 'dad facts!' and even point out places where young animal fans can spot wildlife – squirreltastic!

Plus, there's all the essential info you need to plan a perfect day out – how to get there, where to start, how long to allow – and we've included a map of each route to take. Several walks have more than one route, offering adventures of differing length or difficulty.

In the following pages we give a few tips about what to take on your travels, so if you're new to the buggying experience you'll be starting out on the right foot.

The result: 50 unforgettable family adventures right in the palm of your hand, ready for you all to enjoy as you explore the world together. So, without further ado, we wish you many hours of exciting outdoor escapades and just hope that you have as much fun doing them as we did.

ready to roll?

Before you set out into the brave new world of buggyable walks, there are a few things it's good to know. But this isn't about loading your car with kit. We've selected the walks in this book to be accessible as well as adventurous. So, with just a little prep, you can roll out in total confidence that you'll have a day out to remember.

which buggy?

We have included walks for every type of buggy, although the majority are aimed at all-terrain pushchairs (ATPs).
However, since the amount your wheels/abs can tackle is very much an individual thing, we think it's better to give you as much plain, honest information about the going on the walk and let you make your own mind up. See How to use this book, p13, for more details.

punctures

We did every walk in the book and dozens of others as well and didn't get a single puncture. The last time we did blow a tyre was in a shopping centre.
So, while we would always recommend that you go prepared, it's worth keeping things in perspective. The longest walk in the book is six miles, so you will never be more than three miles from your starting point. If that seems a long way to limp back with a flat, then take a puncture repair kit, tyre levers and pump. But you will have less room for a picnic...

all—weather walking

A wise person once said, 'Britain doesn't have a climate; it has weather', and you don't need us to tell you that conditions can change markedly in a day. But it's worth remembering that this is doubly so in some of the remoter places that this book will take you to. So please remember your waterproofs and your buggy's plastic cover, if it has one. And if it's been raining a lot, wellies are a good idea. We have identified specific walk sections where it can get boggy in winter.
It's also important to think about your little ones' clothing. If they're very small they will be just sitting still as you do all the effort, so will feel the cold – and particularly wind chill – more than you in winter.
The converse is true in summer – you don't want them wrapped up too warmly on a fine day. And please, please, remember to take hats and a good sunscreen. All the lovely wide-open spaces, fresh breezes, and light bouncing off water and sand will soon increase the rosiness of young faces.

food

What with remembering food and milk and nappies and wipes and spare clothes and the thousand other things you need for Junior, it's easy to forget about yourself. Because while knackered kids will eventually zone out in the buggy, you're the one who has to push them back to the car. This is hard and frustrating to do if you are hungry. You need flapjacks!
Seriously, always make sure you have a good stash of yummy things for every member of your party. Also remember to take plenty of water and, if you're out in the winter, a flask of something hot is easily stashed on a buggy's shopping shelf. Top tip – we find a beefy drink or made-up stock cube to be more invigorating than coffee or tea.

how to use this book

timings

It can be tricky to predict how long a walk will take. People go at their own pace and like to rest for different periods. Add in a kid or two and the number of variables increases rapidly: type of buggy, age of child, fitness, nappy/milk/food breaks, strop stops...

But you need some sort of guidance if you're to plan your day successfully. So we have given a range of times for each walk. And how did we work these out?

Average walking speed is 3 miles in an hour. Pushing a light buggy round a well-surfaced track, you might average 2–2½ miles in an hour. A larger buggy, laden with lunches, drinks and waterproofs, will slow you down more and, of course, you have to allow a certain buffer for looking after children and enjoying the scenery. You also need to factor in the condition of the path surface and the gradients.

Since it's far better to err on the side of caution, we have allowed for a walking speed range of 1¼–2 miles per hour and then added an extra slice of time depending on the conditions along the walk itself.

Researching the walks, there were two of us (reasonably fit, but not athletic), pushing a two-year-old in an all-terrain pushchair, stopping for a few minutes every half an hour, and we generally did the walks in the middle of the time range we've provided in these pages.

As you and your family do a few walks yourselves, you'll get to know where your pace fits into the range, which will help you to plan future outings more accurately.

symbols

We've used the symbols below on each of the 50 routes as a general guide to the suitability for buggy types.

 Can be done by virtually any buggy.

 Might be beyond small-wheel pushchairs.

 Only suitable for more rugged buggies and all-terrain pushchairs.

As a walk might be 90 per cent easy-going, but then have a 20-metre forest section that's a little rougher, we've provided explanatory notes about what to expect too. That way you can make up your own mind about whether or not your buggy is suitable for that particular walk.

obstacles

Most of the walks in the book have no steps, stiles or kissing gates. But sometimes a spectacular walk is worth a quick lift up a handful of steps. Where this is the case, we have mentioned the obstacle in the **route** text. But often we offer alternative routes that don't involve the obstacle.

route options

Several walks have more than one **route**. Distances, timings and the going underfoot are given for each to help you plan.

maps

The maps in this book only show the main features of the walk. When used with the **route** text they will give you a clear indication of the path to take, but they do not take the place of an Ordnance Survey map.

We have included a 'getting there' section that directs you to the start point, from where the **route** kicks off. There is also an **OS grid reference** for every walk.

map key

Grass/pasture/moorland

Forest/shrubland

Water

Beach

Built up

Buggy walk **route a**

Buggy walk **route b**

Buggy walk **route c**

Road

Local access road

Other footpath

○   Point of interest

P   Parking

Railway

Cliffs or steep slopes

214
▲   Summit and height

River

rest and refresh

It's good to know where you can find your nearest coffee hit and somewhere you can change a nappy, so we have included details of family-friendly places to eat and drink, and decent loos. Our listings are not exhaustive. A few of the more rural walks have no facilities on the route itself; where this is the case we have pointed out the nearest places to go.

Mind you, it has to be said that one of the best places to change a baby (or enjoy a homemade flapjack) is on a grassy riverbank with the blue sky above you and the butterflies dancing around your head.

further info

To help you plan your walks as part of a holiday or family get-together, we have included the web addresses and any other useful contact details of extra sources of helpful information that are available for each walk. Many of these provide details of places to stay, transport options and other things to do in the area.

walk locator

south west

carbis bay to st ives

A jewel among seaside towns, St Ives bursts with natural charms, and creative spirit flows down every street. You'll find beaches, boats and a million ways to fritter away a day.

St Ives is a work of art. Nature laid the background canvas with a magical turquoise seascape and sandy bays ice-cream-scooped out of a rugged headland. Then humankind did a pretty good job of the detail; our white houses clustering together like seabirds on a rock, leaving only tiny and twisted streets between them. Add the myriad multicoloured shops and people peppering the golden sands while a scattering of boats bob in the harbour and – *voilà* – it's a work of genius.

The town's delights drew artists from the 1920s onwards, and for many years the St Ives scene was mentioned in the same breath as those of Paris, New York and London. This level of fame may have faded, but the artists remain. But why would they leave? The light is still wonderful, the town retains its uniqueness and the sea continues to shine its lustrous blue-green. You'll see many artists' studios and shops along this route, and you'll pass Tate St Ives, housing the pick of the pictures and pottery.

It's more popular and polished these days, but much about St Ives remains unchanged. A chat with the chip shop owner reveals she has been serving up succulent cod for 30 years. The putting green has had the same layout since clubs were made of hickory. And beach buckets may have got fancier, but dads still wield them with dogged determination when building wave-defying sandcastles.

This walk starts in neighbouring Carbis Bay, which also happens to have half a mile of ludicrously alluring beach. It then ascends up to a tree-covered cliffside path that stays cool no matter how hard the Cornish sun beats down. Eventually, it drops down into St Ives, where you can weave your way through the jumble of streets and along the harbour's edge. Then it's out onto the headland to find beach after beach modestly revealing its curves. The Tate provides a final flourish of brilliance before you return to Carbis Bay on foot or take the train for a clackety-clack recap of the masterpiece you just enjoyed.

OS map
Explorer 102

how far
route a: 4⅘ miles
route b: 3½ miles

how long
route a: 3–4 hours
route b: 2½–3 hours

how easy

route a   route b

route a: There are several steps up.
route b: Steps are mostly down.

fishy tales

The warm waters around St Ives attract many unusual aquatic species. In July 2007, a great white shark was reported offshore here, while in June 2011, a fisherman claimed that an oceanic whitetip shark attacked his boat. This type of shark usually only ventures as far north as Portugal and has never before been seen at the UK seashore.

dad fact!

The Baulking House on the lane from Carbis Bay to St Ives was once a lookout spot where the 'huer' would scan the bay for shoals of pilchards. It was his job to raise the alert ('huer' comes from the same source as 'hue and cry') so the fishermen could launch their boats and catch the fish.

route a

- From Carbis Bay station, turn left out of the car park and go downhill towards the beach.
- Follow the path between the Carbis Bay Hotel and the Sands Café, going around the hotel and over the railway via the footbridge (steps here and up to the path). Continue on this path, going straight on when it joins a narrow lane.
- After the path crosses the railway, go sharp right down the zigzag slope. Pass the beach café, putting green, station and loos and continue around the front to St Ives.
- Go around the harbour, all the way to the pier and turn left, passing the museum on the left. Continue round the headland from the car park (steps on the north side) and carry on either to the road or down to Porthmeor Beach.
- The Tate is midway along the beach. Take the back streets to the harbour and then retrace your steps to Carbis Bay.

route b

- To avoid most of the 'up' steps at Carbis Bay, get off the train at St Ives and do the town section of the walk before going back along the coastal path to Carbis Bay.
- To avoid the steps on the north side of St Ives Head, visit the top of the hill on St Ives Head and then walk to the Tate through the streets, instead of via the promontory.

getting there

Parking in Carbis Bay and St Ives isn't easy in high season; it's better to use the park-and-ride at Lelant Saltings railway station (**OS grid ref. SW543365**) and then take the train. Alight at either Carbis Bay for **route a** or St Ives for **route b**.

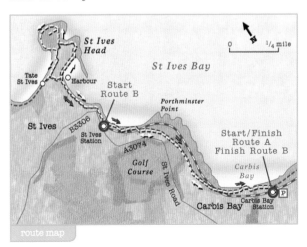

route map

porthtowan

Surfers race into the sea, past kids shaping sandcastles. Waves crash into oblivion on the cliffs, leaving their cloudlike spray in the air. An invigorating Cornish beach walk calls...

North Cornwall's Atlantic shore is famous for its wave-pounded beaches, plunging cliffs and dramatic rocky coves. Bad news for us fans of a mellow buggy walk, right?

Wrong. This is tremendous country for exploring with your young surfer. Okay, the walks around here are a bit more adventurous, but if you throw a tiny bit of caution to the wild west wind then you'll have a day out to remember.

Take Porthtowan. The surf is awesome here (among the best in Europe) and draws plenty of blonde-haired board-heads. But the village is miniscule compared with Newquay, a few miles up the coast. This is largely thanks to Mother Nature – steep-shouldered cliffs ensure that there's just no room for any unpleasant development.

The tide comes up a long way, right past the foot of the cliffs, which has a downside – you can't walk along the beach when the sea is fully in. However, when the tide isn't fully in (which is most of the time), the sea leaves wide miles of white sand so firm you'll want to put a sail on your buggy and speed along land-yacht style.

Walk a golden mile beneath the cliffs to reach Chapel Porth, a nook in the rocks similar to Porthtowan but even smaller – there's just room for a few cars and a beach café here. Once you've had a rejuvenating ninety-nine, you could simply skim back over the beach, but to get the best views (and give your abs the best workout) you'll want to return along the cliff. It's a steep and rocky push to the top, but it's over quickly and puts you at the start of a rollercoaster run along the edge of the country. Heather and bright wild flowers pattern the hillside as the beach soars beneath your feet. Cliff after cliff cascades into the surf in the distance and seabirds wheel below you.

Quite often the people you meet here wear a grin from ear to ear at the sheer wonder of it all – don't laugh at them; chances are you're beaming with the same childish glee.

OS map
Explorer 104

how far
2⅘ miles

how long
2–2½ hours

how easy

The firm sand on the beach is easy, but the push up onto the cliff is hard and very much for ATPs only.

surf's up
Older children will love a surfing lesson from one of the surf schools at Porthtowan. They offer half-day, full-day and weekend courses. Ageing dads who still have what it takes, my lad, are also more than welcome.

dad fact!
The buildings and chimneys perched on the cliff above Chapel Porth are the remains of Wheal Coates. 'Wheal' is Cornish for 'mine' and in 1881 more than 130 people descended into the cliff here every day to dig at a seam of tin just below sea level. Today, its eerie buildings are maintained by the National Trust.

route

- You MUST check the tide times at the start of this walk. They are usually displayed on a board near the car park, or you can ask one of the very cool young RNLI lifeguards on the beach (in summer), who will be delighted to help.
- From the car park, pick a path through the soft dunes towards the sea.
- When you reach the firm sand simply turn right and walk north-west for a mile, until you reach Chapel Porth.
- Walk inland through the car park, past the café and up the little valley a short way to pick up the path that climbs the hill on your right.
- Follow this to the top and then walk back along the cliff towards Porthtowan.
- On the cliff, please stick to the path and if it's truly blowing a gale, return along the beach.
- Note: Dogs are banned from the beach from Easter Sunday until 30 September inclusive.

getting there

Porthtowan is at the end of a network of roads heading coastward from the A30 near Redruth. If coming from the north, the best road to take is the B3277 towards St Agnes, turning left to Porthtowan after 1¼ miles. From the south, take the B3300 that goes to Portreath, then turn right after 1½ miles and follow signs for Porthtowan. When you reach Porthtowan follow signs for the beach and park by the public loos behind the dunes, **OS grid ref. SW693480**.

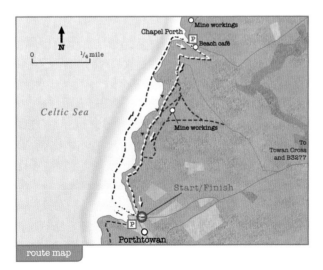

route map

rest and refresh

Blue Bar at Porthtowan is a surfers' hangout that's also family friendly. Its large outside terraces are great for watching the sunset (01209 890329; www.blue-bar.co.uk). The beach café at Chapel Porth does snacks and drinks.

There are public loos at Porthtowan and Chapel Porth car parks.

further info
www.cornwall.gov.uk

perranporth

Leave the crowds behind and wander along a seemingly endless and utterly epic Cornish beach. Then return over a dune-fringed hill for views that'll knock your flip-flops off.

You can see the distant headland as you climb the path through the dunes. Its long finger of rock draws a line at the end of the beach and points far out into the Atlantic. Each notch of crumbled rock and every ocean scar is visible. It feels so close that you could almost reach out and run your own finger along it. The fact it's three miles away proves just how big a natural playground this is.

The walk starts below this lookout point, on the sandy bay in front of Perranporth. Before you start out towards the headland, you'll be tempted to muck about a bit here first. Shacks sell everything you could possibly need for a fun day's play – ice cream, cold drinks, coffee, snacks, inflatable dragons... And the tide really races in, making it perfect for moated sandcastle mayhem.

This little beach certainly is a pleasurable place to be. But those three extra miles of sand will soon call you on. As you head round the small outcrop that encloses the bay you'll see them stretching away before you. Your bare feet will be pawing at the sand; your buggy wheels revving.

There's plenty to see as you go – birds, boats and boarders. The surfers will be out no matter what the weather: the novices skimming in the shallows and the would-be pros bobbing patiently further out, scanning the swell for the tube that will carry them into heaven.

So take a packed lunch and go exploring. You can always turn around when you get tired. On your way back, save some energy for the little loop up onto the outcrop. It's a steep but smooth push up, and the views of the sweeping sea are sensational. And then you drop back down to the last treasure: the UK's only bar on a beach snuggles into the dunes. With its spacious interior, wood and stone exterior and accompanying wide apron of large outside tables, it could easily be some fancy French ski resort's restaurant. Time your return just right and, as you sip your shandy, the sunset will leave you speechless.

OS map
Explorer 104

how far
2½ miles

how long
1¾–2 hours (plus beach fun time)

how easy

The sand is generally firm. The push up onto the headland is on a ramp, but is steep.

a buried treasure

The name Perranporth comes from the Cornish for 'St Piran's cove'. St Piran is the patron saint of Cornwall (and tin miners) and he founded a church near Perranporth in the 7th century. It was lost under the sand for hundreds of years before its ruins were discovered early in the 20th century and became a popular attraction. Unfortunately they were often vandalised, so were once again buried beneath the sands in 1980.

dad fact!

Sand dunes run inland from Perran Beach for almost a mile. Known as Penhale Sands, this area is a haven for wildlife, including the rare Silver-studded Blue butterfly. Somehow Mother Nature manages to co-exist peacefully with the army training camp that also occupies the dunes.

route

- Important: The tide comes in quickly here and you MUST check tide times before setting out. They are posted by the beach, or you can ask a lifeguard.
- From the car park, walk down onto the beach and out towards the sea.
- Bear right and head past the promontory and along the beach for as long as you feel like.
- On your return, go up the zigzag ramp by the surf shack at **OS grid ref. SW758556**.
- Go right, up the little road to just before the entrance to the caravan park, then turn right.
- Follow the broadest path across the hilltop, then down the other side at the edge of the golf course.
- Continue along the path as it curves inland and downhill to the back of the dunes.
- Pick a route through the dunes back to the beach.

getting there

Heading northbound on the A30, take the A3075 at Three Burrows roundabout and follow clear signs to Perranporth. If going southbound on the A30, take the B3285 for Goonhavern and follow signs to Perranporth. Park at **OS grid ref. SW756543**.

rest and refresh

The Watering Hole at Perranporth Beach is good (01872 572888; www.the-wateringhole.co.uk). There are many other cafés in Perranporth town.

There are also public loos up on the south-west headland.

further info

www.perranporthinfo.co.uk

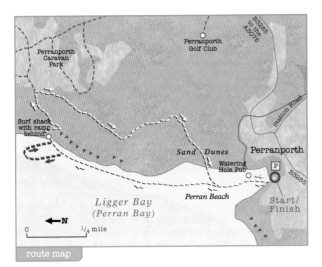

padstow to rock

After a ferry trip to the holiday hangout of rock stars and royals, this walk eases over smooth sands and calm coastal paths. Less rock, more roll. Finish with fish 'n' chips.

The refined eateries, elegant streets and designer boutiques of Padstow and Rock bring the great and the glamorous flocking to this Cornish corner. But to find the true soul of this place you need to walk by the water.

When the ferry skids onto the sand at Rock's beach, you'll start to get the idea. The golden strand curves ahead of you towards the ocean, bound by green dune grass on your right and the blue waters of the River Camel on the left. Above, it's just the open sky. And dotted randomly about this meeting ground of elements are boats, birds and blithe people squeezing the sand with their toes.

Opposite, a scimitar of sand cuts into the estuary, its clean lines belying a darker nature. This is the Doom Bar – a notorious ship-wrecking sandbank. But our little beach is safe enough, and you'll soon find yourself snaking round to Trebetherick. Sir John Betjeman spent much of his life ambling thoughtfully through the dunes here, and he rests in the tiny churchyard at St Enodoc, which you will pass along the way.

There are certainly lots of sandy paths to wander down (no stiles, though) and his inspiration is plain to see. As you round the rocky headland past Trebetherick, the view opens out to the steep cliffs of Stepper Point. Below your feet, waves rush gurgling up tiny inlets towards the rocks. Hidden coves dot the headland with family beaches where generations can idle away a whole holiday.

The far point of the walk is the broad bay of Polzeath, now the province of the wave worshippers. There weren't any surfers when Betjeman first came here, but perhaps they appreciate the heart of this place as much as anyone.

Finally it's back through the dunes to the ferry and Padstow, where you can pick up a seafood supper and sit on the seawall. There you can watch the sun go down as your spirit soars into the blue.

OS map
Explorer 106

how far
6 miles

how long
4–5 hours

how easy

The coastal path from Trebetherick to Polzeath is easy, and the push along the firm sand from Rock is not too hard, but the short section through the dunes from St Enodoc back to Rock can be hard going.

what's in a name?

Rock is named after a nearby quarry, which provided ballast for sailing boats that unloaded their cargo at Padstow. The quarry is now a car park. 'Rock' might seem like an odd name, but then the next two villages are called Splatt and Pityme.

dad fact!

The beautiful church of St Enodoc has nestled in the grassy dunes behind Daymer Bay since the 12th century, but 600 years later it was nearly submerged in drifting sand. It was restored in the 19th century and is once again a place of worship. Former poet laureate Sir John Betjeman is buried in the churchyard.

route

- Note: If the tide is completely in, you won't be able to walk the section all the way from Rock to Trebetherick. You can either start at Trebetherick or simply spend a little time exploring Rock or mucking about on the beach before walking. Please check the tide times in the Tourist Office by Padstow's harbour.
- From Padstow take the ferry over to Rock.
- Walk along the beach all the way to the car park by the beach at Trebetherick.
- Follow the coastal path round to Polzeath.
- Retrace your steps to Trebetherick, then turn inland through the car park and, after 150 metres, take the footpath on your right to St Enodoc Church. (Take care when crossing the golf course.)
- After visiting the church, continue on the path marked by white stones through the golf course.
- Take the path signed for the beach – not Rock – and stay on the broadest track, passing through the dunes and out onto the firm sand of the beach and back to the Rock ferry.

getting there

From the A39 west of Wadebridge, take the A389 signposted 'Padstow'. It's best to use the Padstow park-and-ride. The Rock ferry goes from the harbour (**OS grid ref. SW921755**) or at low tide from the beach 500 metres to the north (steps down). To do the walk from Rock or Trebetherick, take the B3314 from the A39 just north of Wadebridge and follow signs to either place.

rest and refresh

There are dozens of great places to eat and drink in Padstow and Rock; some can be pricey. Alternatively, visit the Surf Lounge at Polzeath's Tubestation (01208 869200; tubestation.org). It has the best-value food and drinks in the area (organic and fair trade focussed), as well as board games, beanbags, a Nintendo Wii, surf movies showing daily, a skate ramp in the coffee shop and they don't even mind if you bring your own food and drink. Talk about cool... In Padstow, Stein's Fish & Chips shop on South Quay is justly famous (www.rickstein.com).

There are public loos at Padstow, Rock, Trebetherick car park and Polzeath.

further info

www.padstowlive.com

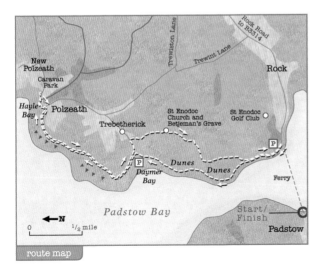

route map

luxulyan valley

When the wind blows wild on the coast, come to Luxulyan's quiet, sheltered valley. You and your family will probably have the trees all to yourselves in this natural oasis.

'Luxulyan Valley' sounds just like a peaceful place to walk (either that or a very fancy brand of soap) – and you'll be pleased to discover that this is not false advertising.

It may still surprise you, however, because this is not the sort of landscape usually associated with Cornwall: a pristine ravine with quiet forest paths and hidden rivers. But if the wind is giving the moors a scouring or the beaches are a little on the busy side, come to this verdant valley and you can be guaranteed a soothing afternoon.

Luxulyan is part of a Cornish Mining World Heritage site, and there's plenty of industrial archaeology on display. The walk alternately follows 'leats' – artificial mini-canals built to harness the power of water – and old tramways. But humankind ceded its dominion long ago and the trees now rule the valley, giving it an unworldly atmosphere.

Soon after your stroll begins along the level path that flanks the first leat, you go under the great Treffry Viaduct. (Almost 200 metres long and towering 30 metres above you, it was built to carry the railway that served local mines and quarries.) After winding through the trees for a while you come past the setting of a huge old waterwheel. The wheel itself is no more, but water still flows through the gap, arcing into fresh air in a proud little cataract that makes a spectacular sight. You then climb gently to the path above it for glimpses through the forest canopy of the wider valley – it's trees all the way!

The same path loops back to bring you over the top of the viaduct, which you can now see is also an aqueduct – one of the leats runs beneath the flags you're standing on. As a finale to your walk you can play what has to be the world's longest game of Pooh Sticks. At the far end of the viaduct there is a wide gap where you can easily drop sticks into the slow-flowing water. Then simply scurry back and wait for your victorious twig to appear at the gap on the other side. Repeat until happy.

OS map
Explorer 107

how far
2⅗ miles

how long
1¾–2 hours

how easy

Mostly easy going on gently sloping tracks, but there are rocky bits and some paths can get muddy. Bring wellies.

wheelly powerful

The waterwheel was built in the 19th century to wind wagons up the 1 in 10 Carmears Incline using a wire rope. It was replaced by an even bigger wheel a few decades later, which powered china clay mills. You can still see granite sleepers from the tramway embedded in the ground of the incline.

dad fact!

Luxulyan is part of the Cornwall and West Devon Mining Landscape, which is a UNESCO World Heritage site. In the 19th century, Cornwall and West Devon produced vast quantities of metals and minerals, including most of the world's output of tin, two-thirds of its copper and half of its arsenic.

route

- Go through the car park and bear left, climbing the handful of steps to an embankment holding a leat.
- Follow the path that runs alongside this for ¾ mile, going underneath the viaduct.
- Pass the old waterwheel pit and continue for 120 metres, after which an old tramway joins from the left.
- Keep going until you reach an old stone bridge, then retrace your steps and take the tramway as it branches uphill to the right.
- You now walk above the waterwheel on a leat-side path above and parallel to the one you walked earlier.
- Follow this track all the way to the viaduct. Cross this to enjoy the views, then return over the viaduct and turn left, following the path to a country lane.
- There is a small step here, then walk down the road to the junction by the car park.

getting there

From the A30 south of Bodmin, take the A391 heading towards Bugle and take the second left, following signs for Luxulyan. Go through the village and continue for ¼ mile, parking on the left in the woods just after a junction with a minor road, **OS grid ref. SX058573**.

rest and refresh

There aren't any facilities along the walk, but there are public loos in Luxulyan village. The Kings Arms pub there has a children's menu, nice outside space and local real ales (01726 850202).

further info

www.cornish-mining.org.uk

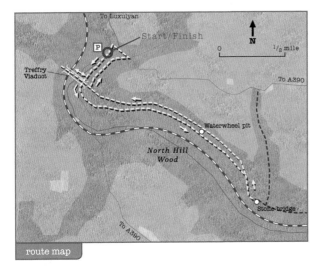

To Luxulyan

Start/Finish

Treffry Viaduct

To A390

Waterwheel pit

North Hill Wood

Stone bridge

To A390

0   ½ mile

N

route map

king's tor

A teasing path invites you out to play on Dartmoor's wide and tempestuous stage, where elemental powers offer a true escape into a wilderness of raw drama.

As you leave Princetown's welcoming cafés behind and strike out into the heart of Dartmoor, you might wonder what you've let yourself in for on this walk. But unless you really can't see your hand in front of your face, it's so worth setting out into this very special place.

As soon as you round the first flank of hillside, Princetown disappears along with any uncertainty you might have felt. Your only thoughts will be concerned with how far you'll be able to explore before your supplies run out – just one more curve, another grand picture...

Within minutes you'll be out in the middle of some of the most beautiful desolation England has to offer. It may not be what you'd call 'pretty', but the scenery here has an epic quality that thrills the soul in a way that rose-covered cottages never quite will.

Moss and marsh stretch for miles and then rise to be capped by the craggy, ruined crown of King's Tor, which our path loops round. Rugged Dartmoor ponies wander by and peer at you curiously from under dew-spangled fringes. Tiny streams trickle through the heather at the very start of their long journey to the sea. Ancient stones mark out endless roads to nowhere. Crumbled quarries tell humbling stories of lives lived by the hardiest of people at the very edge of civilised England.

There's space here in spades – space to think and discover. And since the path is almost completely on the track bed of an old railway, you can forget about route-finding and let your senses run wild in the open vastness of the moor.

The grassed-over abandoned quarries offer myriad perfect picnic nooks. Thousands once hewed granite here, cutting the stone for London Bridge and Nelson's Column. These days, it's just the realm of skylarks and butterflies, but you'll feel stronger for your visit and will return to civilisation with the wild power of the moor in your blood.

OS map
Explorer OL28

how far
5⅔ miles

how long
3–4 hours (although you can turn back at any point)

how easy

Almost no gradient; the going is generally very good, with some pebbly bits. The grassy section through the quarry requires some manoeuvring, but can be avoided.

elementary my dear walker...

Sir Arthur Conan Doyle stayed at the Royal Duchy Hotel in Princetown while writing his Sherlock Holmes tale, *The Hound of the Baskervilles*. In its pages the nearby Fox Tor Mires, a wide expanse of treacherous peat bog, became the great Grimpen Mire, where the hellhound stalked its victims.

dad fact!

The path lies mostly on the track bed of the former Princetown Railway. This was built in 1823 to service the granite quarries, but closed in 1956. The station at Princetown was 435 metres above sea level, making the railway the highest in England.

route

- Turn left out of the car park and pass the fire station, on your left.
- The walk rounds a field then joins the track bed of the old railway.
- Follow this easy path as it skirts the hills. After 1½ miles you pass a detour on the right to Foggintor Quarry. This is worth the extra walk.
- Return to the main track bed as it loops around King's Tor.
- Just after it starts to head south, the track divides – take the left-hand branch and weave your way through the ruins of Swell Tor Quarry.
- The path rejoins the old railway line near the spur to Foggintor Quarry. Turn right and retrace your steps back to Princetown.
- Note: Should the weather turn, you can stop and return the way you came at any point. Likewise, you can continue further along the old railway track, should you wish. Please make sure you take a map with you.

getting there

Follow the B3357 east from Tavistock, or the B3212 north-east from Yelverton, to Princetown. Leave your car at the High Moorland visitor centre, which is signposted from the main road, at **OS grid ref. SX589735.**

rest and refresh

The Fox Tor Café in Princetown offers hearty home-cooked fare, a warm welcome and sofas beside an open fire. There's a family area with toys, too (01822 890238; www.foxtorcafe.com).

There are public loos in town and the High Moorland visitor centre has lots of local information.

further info

Visitor centre: 01822 890414; www.dartmoor-npa.gov.uk

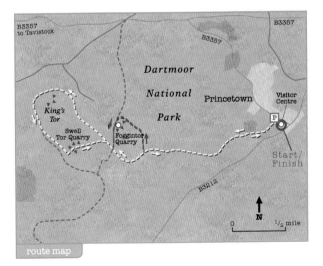

route map

salcombe

Beaches, boats and beautiful people – you'll see them all on this trundle through Devon's popular seaside town. And for the return leg you take to the waves on a fresh ferry ride.

You don't have to be dressed bed-head to loafers in Jack Wills (although the original shop opened here, on Fore Street) to enjoy a day out in Salcombe. Rather than cruise with the yachting set, you could simply hang with the mooching-about-and-soaking-up-the-atmosphere gang – which is just as much fun and a lot less expensive. Which is what this walk is all about – taking us right through the heart of the town and via a couple of golden beaches too.

Luckily, despite its popularity, Salcombe still has sailfuls of charm. This is the kind of town where every corner throws up a new surprise: fishmongers that don't just sell crabs, but also buckets and bait so you can catch your own; mad little alleys that sprint away from the high street like startled cats and then end abruptly in a two-metre drop to the sea; and an RNLI museum with a world-class photo collection of bearded men in woolly jumpers.

The fresh produce available in town is mouthwatering. It's not just a great place to buy seafood; there are excellent bakers, butchers and more coffee shops than you can shake a croissant at. Most are independent too.

Salcombe is famous for its boat-building, an industry that continues to thrive. Most of the workshops are packed together on Island Street, which you'll pass along the way. Many craftsmen still build wooden vessels and often leave their doors open, allowing you a glimpse into their craft.

The walk starts and ends at North Sands, one of the little sandy beaches fringing the town. It's easy to spend a fun few hours here and, as the sea often comes up very close to the rocks, dads can build many an anti-tide fortification.

There's so much to see and do on this route that the return journey is best done on the ferry that zips between the slipway in town and North Sands. You can also catch a boat over to the eastern side of the estuary to explore the necklace of small sandy coves adorning the shore there.

OS map
Explorer OL20

how far
2 miles if using the ferry for the return leg; 4 miles there and back

how long
1½ hours each way. Add an extra 45 minutes for the walk to Lower Batson and an extra 20 minutes for the ferry.

how easy

Hilly in places, but the going is smooth tarmac all the way.

salcombe rocks

Salcombe's stylish streets and refreshing sea air have attracted many celebrity residents. The town has been home to Kate Bush, Sir Michael Parkinson, Alan Titchmarsh, Sir Clive Woodward, Geri Halliwell, Rod Stewart and, at one heady time, most of Led Zeppelin.

dad fact!

The sea floor around Salcombe is littered with shipwrecks, including one of only three known Bronze Age ships in Britain. There is also a 17th-century ship that held a cache of 400 Moroccan gold coins, and HMS *Untiring*, a World War II submarine that was sunk in 1957 for use as a sonar target.

route

- From North Sands beach, take Cliff Road and follow it into town until it becomes Fore Street.
- Pass through town until you reach Island Street, which bends sharply left. It's worth walking past the car park, along Batson Creek to the benches at Lower Batson for a little quietness.
- Then return to the town and either take the ferry (accessed down an alley on Fore Street) to South Sands and walk up and over the steep hill to North Sands, or simply retrace your route through town.
- Note: Most of this walk is along roads and, although pedestrians very much have priority in the narrow Salcombe streets, please keep a sharp eye out for cars when on the more remote stretches.

getting there

From Kingsbridge, take the A381 towards Salcombe. Half a mile after the road enters Salcombe it divides three ways; take the right-hand street, Sandhills Road, and follow it down a series of hairpin turns to reach the parking area behind North Sands beach, **OS grid ref. SX730383.**

rest and refresh

You'll pass many cafés and shops throughout the walk.
The Winking Prawn at North Sands does great barbecued seafood platters to share – and it has a sandpit (01548 842326; winkingprawn.co.uk).

further info

www.salcombeinformation.co.uk

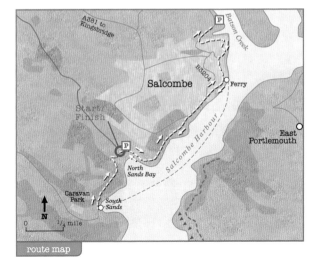

route map

slapton ley

Explore the leafy, wildlife-rich banks of the south-west's largest lake, which happens to be beside a beautiful beach. One of few walks with birds, butterflies and bodyboarders...

As you saunter along the narrow spine of Slapton Sands, you'll see that this is a beach with a split personality. On one hand, it's a steeply banked strand of pebbles enduring a merciless pounding from the waves of Start Bay. On the other, it's the low border of a calm lagoon where dragonflies hover among the silent reeds.

The lagoon is Slapton Ley, a National Nature Reserve and Site of Special Scientific Interest. This one-and-a-half-mile-long lake is freshwater, not salt, and the creatures that inhabit it are very different from those you might expect to find by the seashore.

Shady woodland corners have been allowed to run truly wild, providing a leafy haven for dozens of butterfly species. If you come in autumn, the hedgerows might look like a gardener's nightmare, but you'll be able to pack your lunchbox with fruits, nuts and herbs to take home.

You're barely out of the car park before you reach the first point of interest – a wooden hide. This isn't just the preserve of keen birders, so it's well worth bringing your binoculars and that dusty old bird guide off the top shelf.

The Ley is like Watford Gap services for all sorts of wintering birds en route to warmer climes, and you could see swallows, whitethroat and sedge warblers among the visitors. In summer, the shingle ridge pulls on a dreamcoat of wild flowers, including yellow-horned poppy and the very rare strapwort. The woods around the marshes are also home to badgers, dormice and bats. Don't worry, though, if you don't know your grebes from your coots – one of the viewpoints on the nature walk has the lake's various visitors handily carved into its handrail.

The path heads up from the reserve into picturesque Slapton village. With its romantic ruined tower and medieval church, it's an appealing place to stock up on refreshments for the breezy walk back along the beach.

OS map
Explorer OL20

how far
4½ miles for the whole walk (1⅕ miles for the nature reserve section alone).

how long
3–4 hours for the whole walk (1 hour for the nature reserve part).

how easy

There are some rooty bits in the nature reserve and a few small steps; the path to Torcross is wide but pebbly.

slapton at war
In late 1943 the entire population of Torcross and many surrounding villages was evacuated to make way for 15,000 Allied troops, who came to practise the D-Day landings. There is a touching memorial near the beach remembering this time when war, not today's peace, reigned at Slapton.

dad fact!
During the last ice age the sea was 22 miles from here. Around 10,000 years ago the ice melted and rising sea levels pushed up a shingle beach. By 1,000 BC, a shingle ridge had formed and this held the fresh water back from draining off the land. Slapton Ley was born.

route

- From the car park at Torcross, walk along the path on the crest of the beach towards Slapton Bridge.
- Cross the road and turn left into the nature reserve.
- Follow the yellow 'Village Trail' signs, marked on the walk posts, all the way round.
- After going along a wooden walkway you leave the nature reserve and climb a narrow path that leads through fields towards Slapton village.
- When the lane reaches a junction, turn right and continue through the village.
- Carry on down the road towards the nature reserve entrance and return along the spine of the beach.
- For a shorter walk, park at the nature reserve itself.

getting there

From Dartmouth or Kingsbridge take the A379 to Torcross, where there's a car park, **OS grid ref. SX823423**. If you are only doing the nature reserve walk, park at Slapton Bridge (near the entrance to the nature reserve), **OS grid ref. SX827444**.

rest and refresh

There is a café, a restaurant and a pub with outside seating in Torcross, and also public loos. Fish fans must visit the Britannia seafood shack at nearby Beesands – superyum (08450 550711; www.britanniashellfish.co.uk)!

further info

www.slnnr.org.uk

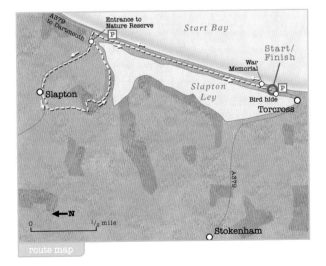

route map

west country

lynton and lynmouth

Explore a fringe of civilisation clinging to the wild edge of Exmoor. Every twist in the path reveals the unexpected – a historic railway, epic sea cliffs, waterfalls and even wild goats.

The twin towns of Lynton and Lynmouth nestle in the towering North Devon cliffs like a pair of broody old seabirds. Although neighbours, they are separated by 150 vertical metres. Fortunately for us, the ever resourceful Victorians built a useful and terrifically fun cliffside railway to link the two. This marks the start of a pair of spectacular walks that can be done independently of each other or together as part of an action-packed day out.

There's an eerie, untamed feel to this nook of the nation. The land seems to shrug its shoulders and then plummet into the ocean. Lush woods flourish in the hanging river valleys. The beach is carpeted with rocks. It feels more like the coast of a Central American republic than England.

One of the two routes (**b**) here is probably the toughest in this book, but its weird wildness is captivating. You start with a ride up the famous cliff railway to explore the crooked streets of Lynton. Then, after a few twists and turns, you're suddenly in a forest, tracking up a steep hillside before popping out of a crown of trees high above a deep gorge. On your left, the houses of Lynton cling improbably to the cliffs while, away to the east, the drop is too steep for any human habitation. You descend through a bracken-floored forest and the first thing you see at the bottom is a huge model railway that an enthusiast has built in his front room. It's free to enter and any Thomas-loving toddler will be entranced.

Route (**a**) is easy in comparison; a mere stroll along a tarmac path. But it still packs the thrills in; traversing a narrow ledge notched into a vertiginous cliff (one of the highest in England). It then climaxes at the Valley of the Rocks, a steep-sided bowl topped with tottering piles of stones. The enchanting oddness is in full flow here: a cricket pitch sits peacefully below the jagged rocks and a tea shop has its hedge trimmed by wild goats. And still you have the return trip on that remarkable railway, with Lynmouth and then the ocean laid out before you.

OS map
Explorer OL9

how far
route a: 2⅖ miles
route b: 2⅗ miles

how long
route a: 1½–2 hours
route b: 2–2½ hours

how easy
route a   route b

route a: Tarmac nearly all the way; exposure is high, please take care.
route b: A hard push on winding paths with some rough sections. ATPs only and best with 2 adults.

romantic getaway

Romantic poet Percy Shelley and his 16-year-old bride Harriet Westbrook honeymooned in Lynmouth in 1812, in the only cottage in the whole town available for holiday rent.

dad fact!

The Lynton and Lynmouth Cliff Railway opened in 1890 and is totally eco-friendly – a stream fills water tanks in the bottom of two carriages. The drivers of each carriage (one at the top of the hill, the other at the base) adjust the water levels until the top carriage is heavier, then release the brakes, and the lower train is pulled up the hill.

route a

- Take the cliff railway from Lynmouth up to Lynton.
- Follow the walled path and turn left on Lee Road, then left again down North Walk, crossing a bridge over the railway.
- Keep straight on this road as it becomes a narrower tarmac path and runs along the cliffside.
- Follow this for just under a mile, until it turns left inland and reaches a road. This is the Valley of the Rocks.
- Turn left, passing the tea room and cricket pitch and head into town, reaching the path to the top of the railway again.

route b

- At the top of the railway (Lynton) follow the walled path to Lee Road; turn left, then right down Queen Street and up the steep hill. At the crossroads turn left, onto the Lynway.
- Follow this to a main road, cross over, past the pub, and cross the river on the stone bridge.
- Turn left and follow the forest path as it climbs Summer House Hill. After the top of the climb take the left-hand path zigzagging downhill all the way to Lynmouth.

getting there

Lynmouth is on the A39 between Ilfracombe and Minehead. The A39 is very steep in places and if you're coming from Minehead please note that caravans are not allowed up Porlock Hill. Park where you can in Lynmouth; there are car parks on the Esplanade, including one at **OS grid ref. SS724495**. The walks start at the lower train station, **OS grid ref. SS722496**. Note: You usually have to fold up your buggy on the railway.

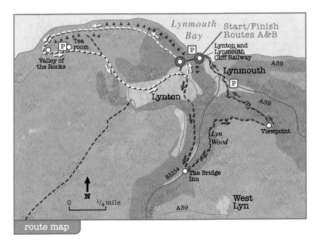

route map

rest and refresh

The Cliff Top Cafaurant at the top of the railway is a great place to stop for refreshment.
Mother Meldrum's Tea Room & Garden in the Valley of the Rocks is also lovely.
There are many other coffee shops and family-friendly pubs in the two towns.

Public loos are at Bottom Meadow car park and by the town hall in Lynton; at Lynmouth's Flood Memorial Hall and Lyndale car park; and opposite the cricket field at the Valley of the Rocks.

further info

www.visitlynton.co.uk
www.cliffrailwaylynton.co.uk

tarr steps

The river takes its time to meander through a wooded valley. You'll want to, too, as you wind gently along its banks, crossing the water by this famed Exmoor monument.

Come here in summer and the scene is idyllic. The River Barle is knee-deep to a toddler, every shining blue-grey stone visible on its bed. The meadow reclines beside the water, exhaling dandelion blooms into the sky. Children scout in the shallows for sticklebacks and splash each other in the deeper pools.

It makes you wonder why anyone went to all the trouble of building the Tarr Steps in the first place. These aren't really steps, but a clapper bridge constructed from large flat slabs resting on upright stones sunk into the riverbed. The bridge has 17 spans stretching for 55 metres, and some of the uprights weigh nearly five tons. It must have been quite an endeavour – especially 3,000-odd years ago.

Visit in winter and it's a spectacularly different scene: the river lashes like a pinned snake, full of floodwater from the Exmoor heights. The Bronze Age locals knew that in order to cross this beast at such times, only a bridge would do – and it would need to be a biggie.

We can be very glad that they made the effort. For most of the year the river is well behaved and the Steps allow us to explore both sides of a verdant valley. Sheltering at the foot of breezy Winsford Hill, this crooked creek reveals its wonders only slowly. So take your time (and a picnic) and just let your wheels lead you into sudden sunlit glades, past rows of foxgloves lining the bank, and alongside horses stretching their necks to sip from the stream.

This woodland is also a national nature reserve, so if you walk quietly you may spot red deer, dormice, bats and even otters. Come in early springtime and you'll be greeted by honeysuckle and bluebells flowering amid the resident beech and oak trunks.

As you return to the Steps, the forest opens out into a flat, flower-laden meadow flanking the river. Here you can just sit amid the butterflies and daisies in a truly unique place.

OS map
Explorer OL9

how far
2½ miles

how long
2–2½ hours

how easy

full walk

east bank only

Can be rooty and narrow in places on the west bank; best done with some teamwork. Going is smoother on the east bank with only the occasional manoeuvre.

rolling stones
In winter the flooded river becomes so powerful that it can wash some of the span stones off their uprights and drag them as far as 50 metres downstream. These slabs weigh up to two tons. They have now all been numbered to make the task of replacing them easier.

dad fact!
Much of the woodland here was once coppiced to provide charcoal for the local iron-smelting industry. Young trees were cut down to near ground level and new shoots would grow from the stump, which would then be harvested one section of the forest at a time, to give a regular supply of wood.

route

- From the car park, go through the obvious gate and take the path downhill, through the field beside the road. This pops out onto the road above the Steps.
- Cross the Steps and turn right along the riverbank.
- Follow this path for nearly a mile as it winds round 4 bends in the river.
- Cross the river by the footbridge and turn right, returning back along the river by the obvious path through the woods.
- Note: the path on the west bank of the river is twisty and rocky in sections, making it only suitable for ATPs. If you want an easier day out, simply stick to the east bank, walking as far along as you wish and returning the same way to enjoy the Steps.

getting there

Head west on the A361, towards Tiverton. Don't go into Tiverton, but take the A396 northbound and turn left onto the B3222 just before Exebridge. When you reach Dulverton, bear left onto the B3223. After 4 miles you will see signs to Liscombe and Tarr Steps down a minor road on your left. Follow this to the car park at **OS grid ref. SS872324**.

rest and refresh
The Tarr Farm Inn, just by the Steps, does good teas and has a terrace with great river views (01643 851507; www.tarrfarm.co.uk).

There are public loos at the car park at the start of the walk.

further info
www.visitsomerset.co.uk

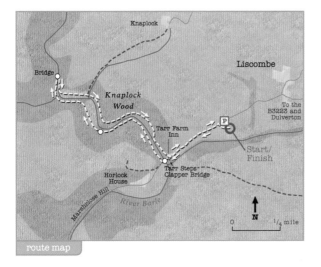

route map

dunkery beacon

You really can stroll up to Exmoor's highest point with a buggy. It's a bold, breezy climb but, so long as the weather holds, this walk will have you grinning between rosy cheeks.

If you enjoyed hillwalking before you had a family, this route will give you a taste of the wild moor freedom and airy mountain adventure that you might have envisaged having to put aside for a few years.

And it isn't as hard as you'd think. There's a bit of height to be gained, but this trail uses shallow gradients and you'll spin to the summit without breaking too much of a sweat. There you can bask in the baffled admiration of the ramblers who came up the steep way.

Scaling this hill gives you a powerful impression of the vastness of Exmoor. There's an otherworldly feel to this land; it's as if Mother Nature built this bit of the model on the wrong scale. As you ascend the track, the hill drops away around you on all sides; its hulking shoulders clad in a mottled coat of heather and wild grasses.

To the south, brooding moor after brooding moor looms into view. Each is tightly cloaked in wooded coombes and laced with sinuous valleys. The occasional hamlet hides among the feet of the hills like a smuggler. And as you crest the wide whaleback ridge, you'll see that the panorama runs all the way north to the ships on the sea and – on the horizon – the rough contours of Wales.

If this epic scenery makes you feel all romantic, you're not alone. This is the setting for R.D Blackmore's classic novel *Lorna Doone*. Standing here, it's all too easy to believe in the notorious Doone clan, plotting their next vengeful act in one of the remote valleys at your feet.

You'll also notice just how many easy-rolling paths there are. They stretch out from the Beacon like the fingers of an open hand, inviting you on to explore more of this sensational countryside. As you amble down from the summit with the whole country spread out before you, plans for new adventures will percolate into your brain. Let them bubble.

OS map
Explorer OL9

how far
3⅘ miles

how long
2–2½ hours

how easy

There are some rocky bits on the path, but the going is generally good considering the location of this walk.

the pickled poet

The nearby town of Porlock has a unique place in literary history. Samuel Taylor Coleridge often came to Exmoor seeking a quiet place to write Romantic verse – and to take opium. He was in the middle of a particularly 'creative' session composing 'Kubla Khan' when he was interrupted by a 'person from Porlock' knocking on his door. He lost his muse and the poem famously stops just 54 lines in.

dad fact!

It's no wonder the views from Dunkery Beacon are so spectacular. At 520 metres above sea level, this is the highest hill in the whole of southern England outside Dartmoor.

route

- From the car park, cross the road and ignore the direct path that leads to the summit; instead take the wide path that heads more obliquely up the hill to the left, in a north-westerly direction.
- Continue for a mile as the path gains height and then turn sharply right on the wide track that leads towards the summit, along the broad ridge.
- From the cairn, drop off the top to the east, heading gradually down for a mile until you reach the road.
- Turn right and walk back along the road to your car.

getting there

From Minehead, take the A39 west towards Porlock. Half a mile before Porlock, turn left into West Luccombe and go on into Horner. Half a mile later, turn right to go up the steep minor road through woods and up onto the moors below Dunkery Hill. The road heads south then south-west around the summit, and then kinks to run south-east – just before this bend there is a small space for parking on the left, **OS grid ref. SS895406**.

rest and refresh

There are no facilities on the route. However, there is a tea room at nearby Horner, and there are several places to eat in Porlock, as well as public loos.
The Café Deli at Malmsmead has a great menu, spacious seating and an outdoor area.

further info

www.exmoor.com

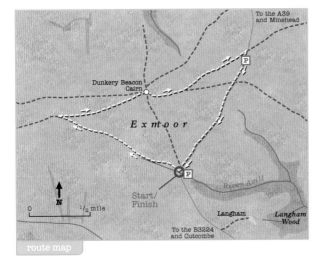

route map

cothelstone hill

With its fine views across cider country, rich wildlife and a slap-up café just down the road, it won't take wild horses to drag you up this hill. But there are a few wild horses too...

Cothelstone Hill resembles a huge knuckle, the last in the line of the clenched fist that is the Quantocks. And certainly the view from the top packs a terrific punch. Bounded only by the sky, it swirls in a full circle about you, from the Brendon Hills and Exmoor in the west, to the Blackdown Hills in the south, Glastonbury Tor in the east and Wales' Gower Peninsula in the north. Between these compass points the earth flows in a swathe of infinitely patterned hills, vales and flatlands, and the Bristol Channel cuts its way into the heart of the country.

The vista may be overwhelming, but the buggy walk is simple, and you'll soon feel at home here. There are lots of little paths that wind their way around this hill, snaking in and out of the heather, and it doesn't matter too much which one you take. Just loop round, past viewpoint after viewpoint, marvelling as whole counties open up before your eyes... You don't so much need an OS map as a national atlas to get a true sense of where you are.

The route finishes triumphantly on top of the hill, where a ring of beech trees provides a dramatic photographic backdrop. These are called the Seven Sisters (although now there are six – one was blown down in a storm) after the seven daughters of Sir Matthew de Stawell – head honcho hereabouts in the 14th century.

Usually this is where you'll meet Cothelstone's resident pure-bred Exmoor ponies. They can roam the whole hill, but their favourite spot is around these trees. Perhaps it's the shelter afforded, or maybe they just like the view. They're the closest relations left to the original wild horse, and will wander off warily if you approach them. But the way they look at you with their doleful brown eyes does give the impression that if only you produced exactly the right sort of snack from your pocket, they might be interested. A very fine carrot, perhaps... Or some Polo mints. Then again, they might just be wondering why on earth you need such a bizarre coat to keep you warm.

OS map
Explorer 140

how far
2⅖ miles

how long
1½–2 hours

how easy

Mostly surfaced paths and easy grassy tracks. A few narrow and bare sections.

panoramic peak

Cothelstone Hill is the highest peak at the southern end of the Quantock Ridge, at 332 metres. It has particularly fine 360° views, and with the aid of crisp weather and keen eyes (okay then, strong binoculars), you'll be able to see 14 counties and 150 churches from the top.

dad fact!

In 1956 the Quantock Hills were designated Britain's first ever area of outstanding natural beauty. The area has its own rangers, who look after the land and wildlife. They introduced the wild ponies to help clear the scrub, which keeps the views clear and encourages a variety of wildlife. Birds like skylarks, stonechats, redstarts and yellowhammers thrive here, as well as other creatures such as snakes.

route

- You can follow the Quantock Ranger Service route that goes clockwise round the hill – it's marked by wooden posts topped by green discs displaying white arrows. But we prefer going anticlockwise – the views unfold slightly more epically.
- From the car park, follow the surfaced path through the trees and turn right when the heathland opens out.
- Follow the widest grassy path, which makes a large loop of the convex hill. When you complete your circuit turn left and climb to the top of the hill.
- Follow your wheel tracks back and down the surfaced path to the start.

getting there

Take the A38 towards North Petherton. As you enter this village, take the lane on the right, signed for Goathurst and Broomfield. Don't turn off to Goathurst or Broomfield, but stay on this lane as it rises on the ridge of the hills. After 5 miles you pass the Pines Café, where you need to bear right up the hill. After 500 metres on the left there is a parking area for Cothelstone Hill, **OS grid ref. ST201328**.

rest and refresh

Nothing on the route, but the Pines Café at the crossroads before the car park is very family-friendly and has a children's play area (01823 451245).

further info

www.quantockhills.com

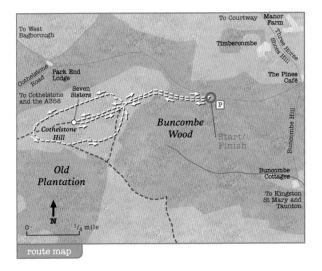

route map

langport levels

Somerset's Levels are an uncrowded land of cider-apple orchards, woods, medieval churches and slow-moving rivers. Amble over its flat plains and spot its hidden treasures.

The Somerset Levels haven't always been an easy place to get about. The area was once a vast marshland, habitable in summer but not in winter, when the rivers flooded and drowned the land. Indeed, the county's name comes from 'sumer saeta' – the land of the summer people.

Much land was drained in the Middle Ages, and by the 18th century a network of ditches, known locally as rhynes, and navigable rivers had transformed the flat land into farms and orchards. Langport became a trading hive and, although the railways later took the river-based trade away, the town's former wealth is evident in its fine architecture and restored wharfs and warehouses.

Today it's a landscape that's perfect for easy walking and cycling. Great swathes of pasture lie wide open, unveiling distant views to the surrounding hills. Water meadows support many varieties of marsh plants, providing habitats for several animal species. In winter, the moors can still flood, creating scenes of both harshness and beauty.

Our route starts at the friendly Langport and River Parrett visitor centre, the hub for several excellent circular walks. It heads out along hedgerow-hugged lanes which soon offer views that would have a 17th-century Dutch landscape painter scrabbling for his brushes. Then it's off on a cross-country jaunt to Muchelney hamlet to see its charming church and old abbey ruins. You can do a shorter walk without this section, but we guarantee you'll return wanting to do more. If that's the case, you could always think about having a spot of refreshment and then introducing Junior to the delights of cycling. The visitor centre has a variety of toddler-toting bikes for hire.

Visit in early June and you could take part in the Langport Walking Festival. This two-day event has organised walks of 5km, 10km, 20km and even 42km through the Somerset Levels, but the emphasis is strictly on fun, and general mooching about is heartily encouraged.

OS map
Explorer 129

how far
route a: 4²⁄₅ miles; **route b:** 2 miles

how long
route a: 2¾–3½ hours
route b: 1¼–1½ hours

how easy
both routes

Both routes are mostly good going on an embankment and old railway. Bumpy sections over fields and up onto the embankment. **Route a** has a section along a quiet road.

heavenly bodies
Muchelney's church of St Peter & St Paul is a must-visit for dads. Look up at the ceiling in the nave and you'll see that the 17th-century artist got a bit carried away when doing the angels – they all have blithely exposed bosoms...

dad fact!
Next time you're confused by the shenanigans in the financial markets, read *Lombard Street* by the economist Walter Bagehot, who was born in Langport. He explained in simple language why credit crunches happen, how the Bank of England should respond and how ordinary folk can best ride the financial storm. And he did so in 1873.

route a

- From the visitor centre car park, turn left and at the end of the road take the Parrett Cycleway.
- After 150 metres, continue over the drovers' road and follow the track for a mile, until you reach a country lane at Westover Farm.
- Turn left, onto the lane to Muchelney to explore the church and abbey. (Take care along this short section of road.)
- Retrace your steps back to the Parrett Cycleway, continuing up it for ¼ mile to a gate on your right that opens into a path across the fields.
- Take this and then follow the path between hedgerows, across another field and head up onto the path along the riverside embankment.
- Cross the river at the bridge and turn left, following the riverside path all the way back to the visitor centre.

route b

- Follow **route a** directions from the visitor centre to the track, but only walk 500 metres up this, until you reach a gate on your left that opens into a path across the fields.
- Take this path (now follow the last two directions of **route a**).

getting there

Langport is 15 miles east of Taunton and 15 miles north-west of Yeovil. Take the A358 towards Yeovil; turn left after 2¼ miles, onto the A378, and continue to Langport. The visitor centre is on the right as you enter the town, **OS grid ref. ST415266**.

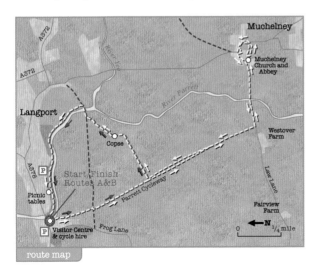

route map

rest and refresh

There are many nice cafés in Langport, including the Parrett Coffee House on the main street (01458 251717).

The visitor centre has loos and a shop.

further info

www.southsomerset.gov.uk

avebury

Strolling through an ancient stone circle is just the start of this adventure. Avebury's fine historical monument also forms the hub of a cracking day's countryside wandering.

Within daytrip reach of both London and Bath, Avebury is easy to get to and yet is off the beaten track. It's the world's biggest stone circle – so large it has a whole village in its centre – but for some happy reason it doesn't attract the huge numbers that Stonehenge does.

This walk introduces you to the circle via West Kennet Avenue, a ceremonial approach that originally had 100 pairs of stones. It's half a mile long and still impressive. As you near the circle, you may be surprised to see that people are wandering freely among the ancient monoliths. This freedom is another advantage that Avebury has over its more famous cousin. Tourists touch them, kids lean on them and wild-bearded men in rainbow trousers do yoga beneath them. Your young ones will love running their hands over the unusual shapes and textures.

Getting up close and personal like this also lets you fully appreciate the awesome grandeur of the site. The stones are ringed by a henge (or raised embankment) and a ditch. These were originally nearly four metres high and 11 metres deep; creating them meant shifting 200,000 tons of rock – using deer antlers as a digging tool. No one is sure why the people of 2500 BC built this monument, but it's clear they had a very good reason for doing so.

Then there's Avebury itself. You might think that having a village amid the stone circle would lessen the monument's majesty, but rather it adds a very English eccentricity. There's a post office and the thatched Red Lion pub (its location unique), built in 1802. This sounds old, until you realise it's 4,000-odd years after the stones were put up.

Our tour of this mystical area concludes with a relaxing stretch through the surrounding fields. Watch out for the strange wooded clumps that dot the horizon. These are Bronze Age barrows (or burial mounds). A landowner in the 19th century planted beech trees on them – it's easy to see why they're now known as hedgehogs.

OS map
Explorer 157

how far
3¹⁄₁₀ miles

how long
2–2½ hours

how easy

Mostly good going, but there are a few slopes to climb, and the path at the field side can be a little rough.

an unlikely saviour

Avebury stood almost untouched until the 1600s, when the tiny settlement in the circle's centre grew rapidly and the villagers began breaking up the stones for building material. It wasn't until marmalade magnate Alexander Keiller bought the site in the 1930s that any real conservation started. He excavated the site and restored many stones to their original positions. It's mostly down to him that the site is as we see it today.

dad fact!

Keiller's workers discovered a skeleton under one of the fallen stones. The man may have been crushed by the stone as he tried to break it up, and was simply left in the grave he'd inadvertently helped create. His purse held a pair of scissors, a lancet and a few coins, so his nemesis was named 'the Barber stone'.

route

- Enter the field to the west of the parking area.
- Walk between the stones up West Kennet Avenue.
- When the road to your right joins the main road, cross the smaller road and walk past the trees to the embankment that runs around the ditch.
- Follow the path on top to your right. When you reach a small road, cross it and continue around the circle.
- At the main road follow the path in, towards the centre of the circle, cross the road and take the path out and around the next sector of the circle.
- Detour to your right to visit the café and visitor centre.
- Join the minor road in the village and walk west to east, right through the circle, passing the pub and the point at which you crossed the road earlier.
- You are now walking away from the circle, down a country lane; continue for ¼ mile, passing Manor Farm, then turn right, down a byway.
- After ½ mile, turn right along the edge of a field. Another ¼ mile will take you back to the start.

getting there

Avebury is on the A361 between Swindon and Devizes, but the best way to approach it is along the A4. Turn onto the B4003 at West Kennet and, after 500 metres, park on the left, in the lay-by beside the start of West Kennet Avenue, **OS grid ref. SU 108691**.

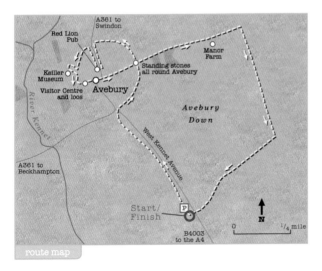

rest and refresh

The Red Lion pub has outdoor space (01672 539266; www.red-lion-pub-avebury.co.uk). The National Trust visitor centre has a spacious café with outside benches. There are loos here also.

further info

Visitor centre: 01672 539250; www.nationaltrust.org.uk/avebury

south

abbotsbury

A winding track leads from streets of flower-decked tea rooms to an airy hilltop lookout. Stand high above the Dorset coast and gaze down the length of an iconic English beach.

Pilgrims have been coming to Abbotsbury for centuries. An abbey was built here in the 11th century and monks sought its sanctuary for 500 years, until Henry VIII got his vengeful hands on it. But the ruin of the abbey didn't stop the peace-seekers. A horticulture-mad countess chose Abbotsbury's forgiving climes for her ideal garden. Sailors steered this way to catch the reassuring landmark of St Catherine's Chapel. Artists drew inspiration from the smuggler-riddled shores – the classic children's novel *Moonfleet* was set nearby – while those who love to ramble have long found solace on the hillsides here.

Today the faithful still come, and within minutes of stepping out of your car you'll understand why: a gentle energy seems to radiate from the town and its environs.

There is also, for such a small place, an incredible amount to see. The ancient abbey's tithe barn is now the centre of the Children's Farm (and is the largest thatched building in the world). The countess's cabbage patch has become a subtropical Eden triumphing at the Chelsea Flower Show. You can even wander amid the descendants of swans once farmed by the resident monks, at the Swannery.

As for the walking, well, the word 'panoramic' doesn't do justice to the awesome vistas that you'll see here. Wind your way up the hill to St Catherine's ancient chapel, and your eyes will be treated to 360° of delight. All around are spread crumpled hills, scattered farms and honey-stoned houses. The extraordinary 18-mile strand of Chesil Beach underlines the scene with a flourish. This is the coast of Thomas Hardy's 'Wessex'; it's easy to imagine a russet-haired heroine here, whispering her dreams to the sea.

And that's where this little journey finishes – an easy track wanders from the 14th-century chapel's hill down to where the sea pounds the myriad pebbles. Take it, and we guarantee you'll return from your Abbotsbury pilgrimage with your spirits truly refreshed.

OS map
Explorer OL15

how far
3⅖ miles

how long
2½–3½ hours

how easy

Mostly easy going, on country tracks. Optional section between a kissing gate and stile. The last few metres of path by the beach are pebbly.

smugglers' satnav

The pebbles comprising Chesil Beach vary from pea-sized, in the west, to potato-like lumps by Portland. Local smugglers were said to be able to tell exactly where they had come ashore on foggy nights by the size of the stones under their feet.

dad fact!

Chesil Beach was created by rising sea levels at the end of the last ice age. It is 18 miles long, 200 metres wide and 15 metres high. It encloses the Fleet: a shallow tidal lagoon that is a haven for wildlife. Storms push it 5 metres inland every century.

route

- From the car park, take the lane to the left of the church.
- Pass under a ruined arch then turn right, onto the minor lane that leads to the village's main street.
- Follow this to the left and, as you round the corner, watch out for the signposted lane on the left.
- Follow this for 300 metres to where the path divides: the main track goes right, while a farm gate with a kissing gate leads straight on to St Catherine's Chapel on the hill.
- You now have a choice: to go straight to the beach, simply bear right on the track and follow it to the shore. Return the same way.
- Or else visit the chapel first and enjoy the views (please do!). To do so, you will need to lift the buggy over the gate in front of you. (There is also a stile to lift it over later.)
- After visiting the chapel, continue towards the sea and then zigzag down the seaward slope.
- Turn right, onto the obvious path near the fence and follow it to a stile.
- Go over the stile and turn left onto a track – the one you left when you went over the gate.
- Follow this track to the sea and then return on it, ignoring the stile and following the track all the way into town.

getting there

Abbotsbury is on the B3157 (accessible via the A35) between Bridport and Weymouth. The car park is beside the abbey ruins, and is signposted from the main street. **OS grid ref. SY578853**.

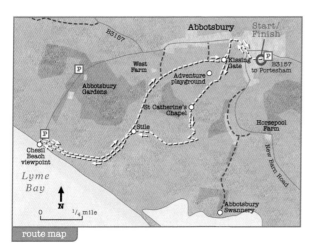

route map

rest and refresh

There are tea rooms galore in Abbotsbury, as well as pubs and public loos.
On the way back into town from the beach there is a truly excellent playground (**OS grid ref. SY574852**) where you can sit while older kids run riot.

further info

www.abbotsbury-tourism.co.uk

durdle door

Stare down at exquisite bays where tiny boats bob on blue waters cradled by sheer limestone cliffs. This is an unforgettable visit to the crowning glory of Dorset's coastline.

Durdle Door is a magical portal that has the power to transport you. Within minutes of starting out on the path to this gem on the gorgeous Dorset coast, you'll feel like you're in another world...

The walk starts with a hard climb up the flank of Hambury Tout, a conical hill standing protectively behind Lulworth. We won't fib – this is slow going, but the steps are shallow and if you take your time you'll soon get into an easy rhythm. Then, when you stop for a break and look back, you'll be astonished at what you've achieved. Far behind you lies Lulworth with its shining cove and emerald fields, as pretty and perfect as a model village. Beyond it, your eyes drift to a wilder land, where the rugged escarpments of the Purbeck cliffs plunge one after another into the sea. You could have your picnic here, but it's probably better to push on because this is just a taster of the startling sea views that lie ahead of you.

Sheer cliffs stand to attention like soldiers, while tiny islands dot the bay. You'll soon be scurrying downhill to see more. The next surprise comes as you pass by – or, rather, 30 metres above – the stunning circlet of Man O' War Bay. Here the waters shift their hue from navy-blue through azure to turquoise, as the deep sea floor shelves quickly up to the beach.

Then Durdle Door reveals itself – this natural limestone arch juts out into the sea, sheltering a beach that sweeps away beneath high chalk walls. The steps down to the shore itself are small, steep and not for everyone. But if you do make the effort, you'll enjoy something special. It's hypnotic to sit on the long bank of smooth pebbles below the cliffs and stare through the arch at the split blue horizon. As the waves suck at the stones you can watch pleasure boats flit across the space it creates in the world.

Returning, you can go through an equally transcendental portal – the entrance to the Lulworth ice cream shop.

OS map
Explorer OL15

how far
2⅖ miles

how long
2–3 hours

how easy

A stepped climb of 80 metres at first; though the going is good and the steps are long and shallow. A rougher track and paths to descend the other side.

jurassic park
Durdle Door is one of the finest sights on a particularly famous stretch of shoreline – the Jurassic Coast. The rocks in this 95-mile stretch of East Devon and Dorset record 185 million years of the Earth's history, making it a Mecca for geologists and young fossil fans alike. The landscape was designated England's first natural UNESCO World Heritage site in 2001.

dad fact!
Durdle Door was formed when the sea eroded softer rocks sandwiched behind harder limestone, creating an arch. Its name is derived from an Old English word, 'thirl', meaning 'bore' or 'drill'. The waves are still drilling – Durdle Door will eventually collapse to leave a sea stack.

route

- Walk to the back of the car park to the gate that leads to the obvious stepped stone path up the flank of the hill.
- Follow this all the way to Durdle Door. Then turn back to return the same way.
- It's possible to return on the other side of the hill (marked on the map with the red dashes) by heading left as you turn back, and going up the gravel track that leads to another car park, near a caravan site.
- Ignore the stiles and continue into the car park until you reach a gate on the right, by a small copse.
- Pass through the gate and follow the path that hugs the fence as it descends east and goes round the hill.
- You will rejoin the main path by the gate from the car park.
- Note: there are no steps on this northerly way around Hambury Tout, so you could go this way there and back for a step-free walk. However, the path does narrow a lot as it skirts the north-east flank of the hill, meaning the route with the steps is simpler – but harder – work.

getting there

From the A352 between Dorchester and Wareham, follow the brown tourist signs from the turning at Winfrith Newburgh if you're coming from the west; follow the brown signs from the turning at Wool if you're coming from the east. Park at Lulworth Cove car park, **OS grid ref. SY822801**. (This can get very busy on Bank Holidays.)

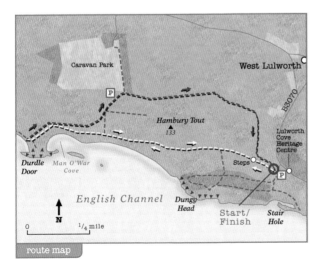

route map

rest and refresh

There are several cafés, pubs and a visitor centre with loos as well as public loos at Lulworth Cove. At busy times a refreshment kiosk visits the track behind Durdle Door.

further info

www.lulworth.com
www.lulworthonline.co.uk

beaulieu to buckler's hard

The wind breathes through the trees. The water laps at wooden palings as sleek yachts slide by. Neat red houses line up on a green shore. Welcome to Beaulieu's quiet beauty.

Beaulieu is a period-film-maker's fantasy; a remarkably unspoiled Georgian village of red-brick houses and cream-painted wood. There are oodles of places to buy goodies such as tea, organic produce and homemade chutney, and if your children have any slightly over-loved teddies, bring them along – there's a bear repair shop in town.

At the heart of Beaulieu's refreshing charm is its river. It might be short (just 12 miles long), but it has more unspoiled reed-beds and tree-shaded glades along its banks than many watercourses 10 times its length. This may be because the entire river is owned by one man: Lord Montagu of Beaulieu. This dominion has allowed the Beaulieu Estate to safeguard its natural treasures wisely – the last major development in the area was around 1780.

For us, this means that a walk from Beaulieu to Buckler's Hard is one of the most refined riverside rambles in the land. You'll sense the special nature of this crook of England before you even start the walk. Near Lyndhurst, you cross a cattle grid and enter the wilds of the New Forest, where ponies and cattle wander blithely about the road as if they own the place. Which, in a way, they do.

The route runs from behind a flower-festooned hotel out into the fields, before meeting up with the River Beaulieu. The path then hugs the bank below the trees, giving you a view of people mucking about in some very lovely boats.

After a turn around a fascinating working boatyard, you pop out at the historic hamlet of Buckler's Hard. This is where the ships that helped build the British Empire were launched, though these days it's hard to imagine the sleepy streets producing much more than an empire biscuit. But that's fine – the tables on the grassy bank by the jetty offer a magical spot for a picnic. While you look over the rippling water running to the sea the wind will soon catch the thoughts of young and old alike, taking them far away to the realm of pirates and discoveries.

OS map
Explorer OL22

how far
4⅗ miles

how long
2½–3½ hours

how easy

Very flat and mostly very easy going; a few rooty bits on the woodland section.

lovely jubbly
Beaulieu is home to the much-loved National Motor Museum. This is one of the world's finest car collections, with more than 250 vehicles that shaped the history of motoring. The automotive treasures on show include four world land-speed record holders, several *James Bond* film vehicles and, most sensationally, Del Boy's yellow Reliant Regal. Cushty!

dad fact!
The plentiful supply of wood from the surrounding New Forest helped make the Beaulieu River a famous shipbuilding centre. In the 60 years from 1747 onwards more than 50 warships were built at Buckler's Hard, including Nelson's favourite ship, the HMS *Agamemnon* in 1777.

route

- From the car park, head to the High Street and turn left.
- Walk round the Montagu Arms Hotel, past the fire station and the hotel car park.
- A gate leads to a straight track that passes between fields. Take this and continue along it, as it bends through a wood and passes through a field, always following signs for Buckler's Hard.
- After Bailey's Hard, the path divides: a forest track goes dead-straight ahead, while a narrower path veers left, towards the river.
- Take the riverside route and continue to follow the signs all the way to Buckler's Hard. For an easier return, take the straight track through the forest.

getting there

From junction 1 of the M27, take the A337 to Lyndhurst then the B3056 (Beaulieu Road) to Beaulieu. There is a small car park in the middle of Beaulieu village, **OS grid ref. SU386022**. Overflow parking is available at the National Motor Museum.

rest and refresh

The café at Fairweather's Garden Centre in Beaulieu does lovely snacks using home-grown fruit and veg, and has a children's play area (www.fairweathers.co.uk). The Master Builder's Hotel in Buckler's Hard has lots of outside space and does great barbecues (08448 153399; www.themasterbuilders.co.uk). There is also a refreshment kiosk at Buckler's Hard.

There are public loos at Beaulieu.

further info

www.beaulieu.co.uk
www.bucklershard.co.uk

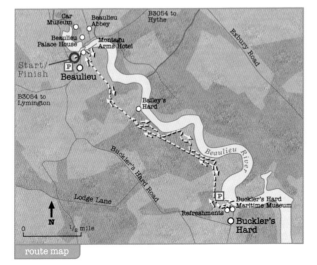

route map

medmenham meadow

Take a treelined lane to a secret path that winds its way to a riverbank fringed with wild flowers – and one of the quietest stretches of England's most famous waterway.

The mass of the metropolis is just 15 miles away and yet here you are, rolling smoothly along the riverside, past gaggles of geese, banks of wild flowers, brightly painted boats and acres of wide-open meadow. The Thames at Medmenham is such an idyllic stretch of water that it's hard to imagine this is the same river that will soon flow by the grey stones of London's embankments.

The only sounds are the gentle putt-putt of boat motors and the twitt-twitt of the birds. In the shallows the water is clear. Rippled sand reflects the sun and the reeds glisten. Pause on the verdant bank and take a closer look – you'll soon see little fish dashing in and out of the shadows. The fishermen who roost at the river's edge will assure you that there are whoppers to be had: roach, perch, chub and bream all love these waters, and you might see a few carp basking near the surface in the summer months. Hard to believe, perhaps, but salmon also swim the Thames waters; these noble fish returned in 1974 – after an absence of 150 years – and have come back here every summer since.

The walk is very simple: follow the river for a while then cut back across the fields. But there's so much to be seen that it will feel like you're having an uncommon adventure. Orchids are generally rare in Britain, but you may very well spot the marsh orchid in these fertile grasslands. At one point you pass a large house on the opposite side of the river, standing stately and proud above the reeds and willows. It's hard not to look at it and imagine Ratty and Mole walking up the bank to visit Toad.

This riverside abounds in those beneath-the-willow-boughs, sun-dappled patches of grass that the cucumber sandwich was invented for – so don't forget to bring along a picnic. You can stick the brake on, kick back and munch your lunch while you watch the herons lurking under the lower-hanging trees, patiently waiting to pick up a picnic of their own.

OS map
Explorer 171

how far
3⅕ miles

how long
2–2½ hours

how easy

Generally very easy path through a grassy meadow, but it is bumpier through the fields. There is a stile to go over, but this can be avoided with a detour.

bedlam at medmenham

Near where the leafy lane leads to the river lies Medmenham Abbey. This once-holy building became notorious in the 18th century, when it was owned by the rakish playboy, Sir Francis Dashwood. He and his friends founded the Hellfire Club and they met here for wild and debauched revelries that often lasted for days at a time.

dad fact!

It was this part of the world that helped stoke the imagination of Kenneth Grahame, author of *The Wind In The Willows*. He spent much of his childhood just round the next turn of the river, at Cookham Dean.

route

- From the parking spot, walk down Ferry Lane until you reach the river, and turn right.
- Continue along the riverside for just over a mile, passing through a meadow and then field edges, until a cottage blocks the riverside path.
- Turn right and walk away from the river for 200 metres, then turn right again on the path that crosses the field.
- After 300 metres, cross a track and second field, then a second track, a third field and then a third track.
- Still with us? Good. At the next field the path splits; take the left-hand fork along the field's edge.
- When you reach the next track go across it and then along a leafy path that will bring you back to Ferry Lane.
- This little section has a stile, but you can avoid this by turning left to go up the last track.
- When you reach the main road, turn right and after 400 metres you'll be back at the end of Ferry Lane.

getting there

Medmenham is on the A4155 between Henley-on-Thames and Marlow. If you're coming from Henley, turn right into Ferry Lane, which is just after St Peter & St Paul Church. Or, if travelling from Marlow, Ferry Lane is on your left before the church. Park on this lane, **OS grid ref. SU805839**.

rest and refresh

There are no facilities on the route itself, but Ye Olde Dog & Badger pub at the top of Ferry Lane has tables outside (01491 571362; www.thedogandbadger.com).

further info

www.visitthames.co.uk

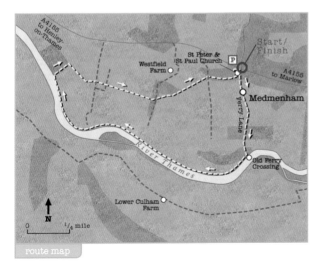

route map

storrington downs

The plumped-up pillows of the South Downs lie above a giant's green bed of countryside quilt, inviting you to climb on up and relax with the fresh air and some unspoilt views.

Next time you're tempted to zoom down to Brighton to see the sea, try turning off when you reach the A272 instead. In a few minutes, you'll be tootling happily through countryside that most folk, when they're travelling through this part of the world, don't even know exists.

Wind your way south west, through quiet villages, until you reach Storrington, and it's here that a magical and mood-altering road starts. It's called Chantry Lane and it begins inauspiciously at the end of the town's bustling high street. From there, though, it winds its leafy way through ever-sparser clutches of houses until, suddenly, it pops right up onto the South Downs, depositing you high above patchwork fields and forests.

The feeling of space you get at the start of this walk is rare for the heart of southern England: here's a pocket of countryside with the same freedom as any wild moor or open fen. Here, little hills have big characters, and the farmland makes a colourful muse for any artist.

Several paths radiate from the car park, then subdivide further to create an enchanted web of walkways that you'll happily be snared by. A farm appears in the distance and, as you slowly roll towards it, you have time to notice how the wide wheat fields sandwich chunky strips of woodland. Gliders as well as birds soar on silent spiralling thermals. Blazing yellow tracts of sunflowers attract equally glamorous bedfellows: poppies, daisies and flax.

If we could liken it to soul food, this walk would be a fresh salad with a zingy vinaigrette and crusty bread straight from the oven. It makes for the kind of day when you'll need a red gingham tablecloth and picnic basket with you.

Oh, and you'll still be able to see the sea, even though it's 10 miles away. And if you look the other way, your eyes will drift along the sinuous spine of the North Downs. But that's a magical road to take another day...

OS map
Explorer 121

how far
5⅕ miles

how long
3½–4½ hours

how easy

Wide farm tracks for the majority of the route. The path narrows for a few hundred metres near the end, but not awkwardly so. The gradients are gentle.

poet's corner
Storrington's peaceful air has attracted more than its fair share of creative spirits. The Victorian poet Francis Thomson came here to write and try to shake his opium addiction. Hilaire Belloc was another frequent visitor, and the sculpting skills of the young Eric Gill can be seen on headstones in the churchyard here.

dad fact!
The walk lies within the South Downs, only recently designated a National Park, in 2011. A swathe of relatively unspoilt down and farmland stretching for 87 miles, from Winchester in the west to Eastbourne in the east, the South Downs National Park is now protected from reckless development by law.

route

- From the car park, head south through the gate signed 'Angmering Park Estate'. Follow the track all the way down the hill and through a gate.
- Bear right and continue past cottages and farm buildings. After a mile you reach a T-junction: turn right.
- Go through another gate, bearing right, and on through double gates to the end of the treeline on the right.
- Turn right, through another gate signed 'Angmering Park Estate'. Cross the field, go through the wooden gate and turn left. Follow the edge of the field, for 300 metres, to a three-way footpath sign.
- Follow the right-hand path through the field. (If the field has recently been ploughed, it may be easier to continue up the field to the South Downs Way. Turn right along this and rejoin the walk later.)
- Pass through another field, a metal gate and onto a footpath crossroads.
- Go straight until you reach the South Downs Way. Continue over this to a T-junction: turn right.
- As the view opens out to the north, turn right at the next junction. Continue along the edge of the escarpment until you reach the road. Turn right, towards the car park.

getting there

Head east along the A283 from Storrington. After you pass Boots on the left, you go over a mini roundabout. The second turning on the right after this is Chantry Lane. Follow this for 2 miles, until you reach a car park on top of the Downs, **OS grid ref. TQ087119**.

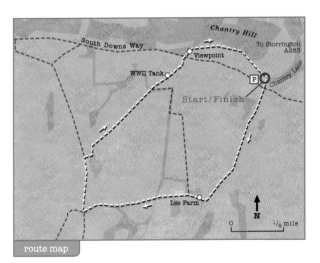

rest and refresh

There are no facilities on the walk, but there are plenty in nearby Storrington, including the Vintage Rose Café & Bookshop, which is very child-friendly. It does book readings for children on Saturday mornings (01903 744100).

further info

www.storrington.org.uk

cuckmere haven

Reach an eye-popping viewpoint, via a low-lying riverside meadow, to stand above the crashing waves as salt air fills your lungs and the stunning Seven Sisters thrill your eyes.

You think you've stumbled upon a perfect country walk: a flat path that meanders beside a leafy hedgerow. Drowsy sheep munch meticulously in gentle meadows. A river snakes lazily beside, flowing off to nowhere in particular.

But then the unexpected happens. As you wander up a shallow slope towards some old coastguard cottages, the larger hill on the other side of the river simply drops away, its skyline disappearing into the sudden blue sea. Walking further, you see that this isn't the only hill to be chopped: peak after peak has been cut off in its prime, to turn the shore into a vertical wave of grooves and curves.

Welcome to the Seven Sisters, a series of sheer chalk cliffs and one of England's most evocative images. This is where the South Downs meet the sea and the highest hill, Haven Brow, drops 77 metres into the waves.

Officially, the Sisters were formed when ancient rivers gouged valleys into the chalk. But, as the glorious vision fires your imagination, it seems equally likely that a giant went berserk here with a huge crinkle-cut chip slicer. Who knows for sure? Either way, it's a dazzling view and on a sunny day the chalk shines with eye-squinting brilliance.

The wander back is a soothing tonic – an easy path along the embankment that keeps the high tide from flooding the low-lying farm plain. The River Cuckmere drifts past on your right, with the occasional canoeist testing their skills on its tidal curves. Meanwhile, in the fields, the sheep chomp absently on, oblivious to their scenic abode.

You may want to visit sooner rather than later. Plans are afoot to stop maintaining the levees and let the sea have its way with the valley. This would mean that eventually the estuary would reflood to create a marshland. Great news if you're an oystercatcher, but this walk would be several feet underwater, so come and enjoy its serenity while the hedges are still leafy and the paths still smooth.

OS map
Explorer 123

how far
2⅖ miles

how long
1½–2 hours

how easy

Almost no gradient; very easy going on a wide track for the majority of the walk. The return path narrows a little for short stretches.

cinematic seascape

Cuckmere Haven is the only undeveloped river mouth in Sussex. The pristine condition of the area makes it a popular film and TV location, and the Sisters often stand in for the white cliffs of Dover. The beach featured in the film *Atonement*.

dad fact!

The Seven Sisters are shrinking. Every year, the constant ravaging of the sea cuts the cliffs back landwards by 30–40 centimetres. You can often see major falls after heavy storms or rough seas. At low tide, you can see metal in the sea near the river mouth. This is the wreck of the *Polynesia*, a German ship that ran aground in April 1890.

route

- Go through the Golden Galleon pub's car park and take the obvious gate.
- Bear slightly right and follow the track that skirts the base of the slopes on your right (the Vanguard Way).
- This eventually brings you to a slope above the old coastguard cottages at the shore.
- Go down, past the backs of the cottages, and along the bank at the top of the beach.
- Turn left at the river, and follow the path on top of the embankment back inland.
- This joins up with the outward track shortly before the car park.

getting there

Drive east from Seaford along the A259. Half a mile outside town the road drops to cross the Cuckmere river at Exceat Bridge. There is a pub here, the Golden Galleon (**OS grid ref. TV513993**). Note that parking here is for customers only, so please have a post-walk beer if you use it! Alternatively, park over the river, to the east, at Exceat (**OS grid ref. TL443588**) – though this will add a further mile to the route.

rest and refresh

The Golden Galleon pub has outdoor seating suitable for families (01323 892247).

further info

www.nationaltrust.org.uk

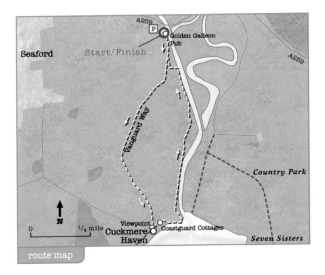

route map

east anglia

cambridge backs

You don't need to be a bright young student to enjoy Cambridge's charms. Come and let its calm green spaces soothe your spirit and the elegant colleges elevate your mind.

Cambridge is a pleasure to explore. The city streets are living history, with every college spire, shop doorway and ancient church telling its own story. There's also a magical escape route into a more tranquil world. Our route takes you through the Backs, a strip of green land beyond the river, near King's and its neighbouring colleges. It starts at one of only four Round Churches in Britain, before embarking on a switchback tour of colleges, bridges and town buildings. You'll pass the university's oldest college, Peterhouse, which was founded in 1284, and see the famous Bridge of Sighs.

The colleges may not have changed in centuries, but this is a walk that's different every time you do it. On winter mornings, a layer of icing-sugar frost dusts the wide swathes of grass, students hurry by in improbable scarves and the chill air crisps your breath into clouds. Come in spring and you'll see the mellow limestone buildings turn the colour of fresh honey in the sun, under a light-blue sky.

It's all change in summer. Most of the students are gone; now gaggles of foreign language students cluster at street corners. Some scholars do stay on to serve coffee, catch up on studies or earn a few beer tokens punting tourists along the placid River Cam. It's worth taking to the water, especially if you also have older children. It'll feel like you're playing the swans at their own game as you ease effortlessly beneath bridges and past drooping willows.

Then there's something magical about autumn here; the undergraduates are at their most diligent, and the treelined paths become a leafy mosaic of golds and browns. There's a whisper of winter in the crisp air.

At the heart of it all is the river, and there are many places to sit down on its banks and simply watch the world drift by. Take a moment to enjoy the peace and you'll see why so many great thinkers have flourished in this bustling and beautiful little city.

OS map
Explorer 209

how far
3¹⁄₁₀ miles

how long
2–2½ hours

how easy

Streets and firm paths throughout.

cow town

Scholars' Piece is the area of the Backs behind King's College. This was the heart of the city in the 15th century, until Henry VI seized the land and razed the buildings to create King's College in 1441. He had to give the town a £26 annual tax break as recompense. Now the area is home to a rather incongruous herd of cattle. The bumps they ruminate over are probably the remains of medieval Cambridge.

dad fact!

Trumpington Street's wide gutters are Hobson's Conduit, a watercourse built in 1614 to provide the city with clean drinking water. Its construction was funded by the same Thomas Hobson who gave his name to 'Hobson's choice': he owned a livery stable and to prevent his best horses being overworked, he offered customers the choice of the horse nearest the door or none at all.

route

- From the Round Church (**OS grid ref. TL448587**), walk along St John's Street then turn right down Trinity Lane, following it as it bends to the left and then taking the small alley on the right, before the entrance to Trinity Hall.
- Go over Garret Hostel Bridge, turn right onto the path just before the road and follow it past Trinity Bridge and along the riverbank to the Bridge of Sighs.
- Return to the path after Garret Hostel Bridge and turn right, crossing the grass to turn left, into Clare College.
- Go over Clare Bridge and into Clare College, through a gate, into a lane, then bear right to head to King's College Chapel.
- Pass the corner of the chapel and head right, along the edge of the green, turning left at the river.
- Cross King's Bridge, go along the path and through the iron gates. Turn left onto the path across the grass of the Backs, and left at Silver Street, continuing over the river.
- Take the alley between the patisserie and the Anchor pub, then turn right, through the gate and back over the river.
- Take the riverside path left, to the main road. Turn left over the bridge and left again, onto a path for the city centre.
- Go right, up Little St Mary's Lane and left onto Trumpington Street and carry straight on, to the start point.

getting there

Parking in Cambridge can be a hassle; it's better to come by train or use the park-and-ride system. If you do drive, there are some convenient parking spots on the Backs at Queen's Road. These run south from **OS grid ref. TL443588**.

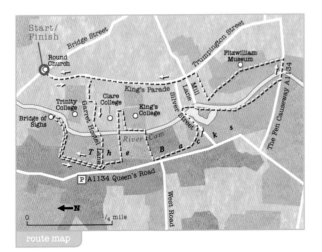

route map

rest and refresh

There are cafés, loos and spots for picnics at many points along the walk.

Livingstones is very child-friendly with good changing facilities: (St Andrews Street; 01223 566030).

further info

www.visitcambridge.org

snape to iken

An opera house sits between river and fields. Nearby, a church stands alone on an outcrop. And the journey between the two is so serene that, even if it rains, you'll be singing inside.

There's music in the air at Snape, that's for sure. To start with, you park at the world-famous performing arts centre, Snape Maltings. Composer Benjamin Britten turned this from a derelict industrial site into a musical Mecca. Every June, thousands flock here for the Aldeburgh Festival, an annual celebration of classical music and the arts.

But there's also a natural harmony beyond the buildings, which you can enjoy on every step of this walk. It's in the tinkling ripples of the waves on the shore; the billow of the wind in the sails of old boats; the rustle of the reeds at the water's edge; the fanfare of bright pink and red flowers lining a country lane... Even the way the walk itself weaves out into the countryside is like a melody.

It's what attracted Britten here in the first place and, once you've explored the Maltings a little, you'll be keen to be off through the fields. Your first discovery will be the weird and wonderful artworks that adorn the grassy flats behind the concert hall. A rabbit in a dinner jacket looks down from a canvas high on a wall. A huge shire horse pulls his load of giant marrows proudly towards the sea. Sinuous sculptures frame the waving reeds. And as you move from farmland to the wetlands at the water's edge, you'll see some of Mother Nature's own artistry – ancient trees weathered and withered into strange shapes.

The path now passes a sleepy picnic spot before sweeping you round the side of a golden-edged beach where the sea shimmers silver on the mudflats. Almost certainly there'll be wading birds here, singing their own plaintive songs.

There's a bustle in the hedgerows at the tiny hamlet of Iken and then, at the turning point of the walk, comes silence. From its stone tower to its thatched roof and grassy churchyard, St Botolph's simply emanates peace. Pilgrims have journeyed here to savour its serenity for almost 1,350 years. Stay a while and enjoy the simplicity before returning to the symphony of Snape.

OS map
Explorer 212

how far
4⅘ miles

how long
3–4 hours

how easy

Varied going including boardwalk, firm beach, country lane and fieldside path.

stinking rich

Before music and before brewing, Snape was renowned for a very different sort of industry – the production of fertiliser from fossilised dung. The local merchant who developed this remarkable process became rich, and his empire became the fertiliser company Fisons.

dad facts!

In 1948 Benjamin Britten co-founded the Aldeburgh Festival in his native Suffolk. Within a few years the event became world-famous and, in 1967, he found a new home for the growing audiences by converting the old Maltings at Snape into an 832-seat venue. Snape went on to achieve even greater fame when JK Rowling named the *Harry Potter* character Severus Snape after the village.

route

- From the car park, pass through the Maltings buildings and follow the signposted path that runs south-east into the countryside. This is the Suffolk Coast Path.
- It continues through fields, over a boardwalk, past a picnic spot and along the edge of a beach before cutting over to join the little country lane that leads to Iken. (There is a handful of steps in the thicket before you reach the lane.)
- When you do get to the lane, turn left and follow it to the church, then return by the same route.
- Note: You can also do this walk as a one-way trip, going or returning by ferry. However, as the ferry service is tide-dependent, you'll need to check the timetable posted on the wharf at Snape Maltings.

getting there

From the A12, take the A1094 signposted towards Snape Maltings. Turn right at Snape Church, onto the B1069, and continue through Snape village before turning left into Snape Maltings, **OS grid ref. TM392575**. You can also get the bus to Snape from both Aldeburgh and Woodbridge. There is a stop outside the Maltings.

rest and refresh

Snape Maltings has a café, tea room, pub and loos.

further info

Snape Maltings: 01728 688303; www.snapemaltings.co.uk

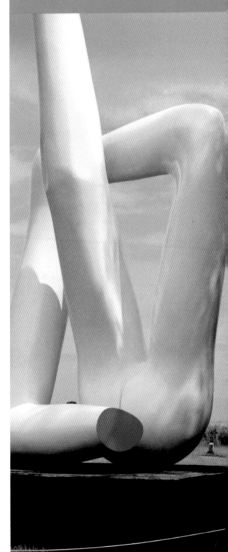

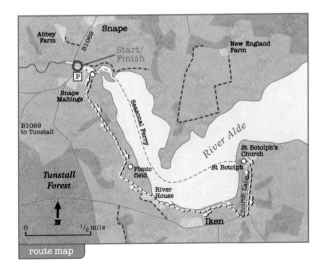

route map

walberswick

Kids pile crabs in buckets, artists set up their easels, the sea pulls relentlessly at miles of sandy shore. And behind it all, a chance to escape into a secret world of reeds and rivers.

At the end of a long East Anglian lane, the little town of Walberswick hides its sleepy cottages amid a thousand acres of coast, wetland and heath that is justly proclaimed as an area of outstanding natural beauty.

Southwold may draw more tourists to this corner of Suffolk, but its neighbour, across the River Blyth, is perhaps prettier. The beach that begins at Walberswick stretches for nearly 10 miles, to Thorpeness, while behind the foreshore is a quiet world of lazy rivers, reed beds and wildlife-crammed hedgerows. The village itself is made up of much-loved cottages, tottering quayside houses and crazy wooden wharf pilings. It's easy to see why this was the centre of English Impressionist painting a century ago.

The walk starts with a cobweb-blowing, leg-stretching push out along the spine of the beach. Here you can watch the sun worshippers and surfers mingle with painters and horse riders on this most cosmopolitan of coasts. But as you turn inland, through the Westwood marshes, you'll see far more birds than you will people. It wasn't always this way – a derelict windmill and the odd wartime pillbox tell tales of busier times – but now this is nature's realm.

There are several footpaths looping and twisting back on each other, so don't worry too much if you wander off track. It's usually easy to connect back up with the path you should be on and if not – ah well, getting lost is often the best way to find new things.

After you do make it back, take time to wander along to the riverfront to grab an ice cream and watch the crabbing. You might wonder why several people are lining up to talk to a woman in a rowing boat. This is actually the official Walberswick ferry. One of the last ferries in the country to be rowed, it has been piloted by five generations of the same family. You'll be whisked across the tidal stream to the Southwold side in a couple of minutes, and the fun detour is well worth the 80p fare.

OS map
Explorer 231

how far
3½ miles

how long
2½–3½ hours

how easy

The path along the back of the beach is generally firm, but pebbly in some places. Vegetation can make paths in the nature reserve narrow at the height of summer.

crab crazy
For over 30 years Walberswick has hosted the British Open Crabbing Championship. Children of all ages can have a bash (the only rule being that nobody born before 1890 may enter) and the aim is simple: catch the biggest crab you can within 90 minutes.

dad fact!
Nearby Dunwich was once one of eastern England's largest ports, but the past few centuries have seen it almost entirely lost due to coastal erosion. The last of the town's original churches, All Saints', reached the cliff's edge in 1904 and its tower finally fell in 1922. The only remaining gravestone – for Jacob Forster, who died in the late 1700s – stands four metres from the cliff edge.

route

- From the car park, head past the huts to the ridge of the beach; turn right and follow the firm path for 1¼ miles, until you reach a signposted path on your right.
- Follow this wide track inland, bear left past a ruined windmill and then turn right at the woods, going over a boardwalk.
- The path loops over a hill in a small wood. Don't take the track towards the houses in the distance, but bear right to stay on the edge of the marsh.
- Take a right-hand turn that leads to the River Dunwich; turn left at this and then cross the river at the little footbridge (there are a few steps here) before rejoining the beach and heading back to the car park.

getting there

Coming up the A12 from Ipswich, turn right onto the B1387, ½ mile before Blythburgh. On the A12 from Lowestoft, turn left onto the B1125 at Blythburgh, then left again onto the B1387. Continue along the B1387 to Walberswick; go straight through the village to the car park that's over a bridge and behind the beach, **OS grid ref. TM499746**.

rest and refresh

Walberswick has tea rooms and pubs, which are welcoming to families, although they can be a little pricey.
The village shop has plenty of picnic supplies.

Walberswick has public loos too.

further info

www.walberswick.ws
www.suffolktouristguide.com

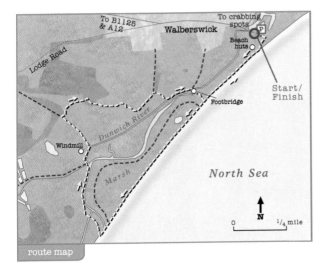

route map

upton dyke

Let the wind fill your sails while you stroll beside the reed-hemmed Norfolk Broads. Old windmills point to the harder-working past of what is now a landscape of quiet leisure.

Life moves at a gentle pace at Upton Dyke. You might even say it cruises. The reason why most people come here is to muck about in boats. Not the kind that go zooming around, but those that idle slowly along the fens, past reeds and ancient windmills, under willows and alongside fields full of sleepy cattle before easing up to a riverbank pub, just in time for a hard-earned spot of lunch.

The dyke itself isn't very long, just half a mile, but it leads to the River Bure, the longest of the Broads rivers that connects with all sorts of other rivers and watercourses, making the scope for water-based fun wide and wonderful.

The walk follows the dyke until it meets the river and, if you come this way in summer, you're sure to see people tinkering with their craft as you pass by; painting the woodwork, tweaking a winch or perhaps just checking that the wine glasses are sound.

Then, as you walk along the River Bure, you may also see a Norfolk wherry easing alongside. Originally built as trading vessels, these stately boats could carry 25 tons of cargo, and had masts that could be dropped to allow the wherry to pass under low bridges. They were made obsolete by the railways, but have since enjoyed a new life as pleasure craft. There is something elegant and effortless about the way they glide through the peaceful Broads. Watch out for their unusual high-peaked sails.

Keep an eye out, too, for local wildlife. The wetlands around the dyke have been designated a Site of Special Scientific Interest, and you're very likely to see plenty of birds probing the marshes for a tasty morsel.

So intoxicating is this quiet corner of the world that you might spend lunchtime at the White Horse pub, hatching plans to get out on the water yourself. So it's worthwhile knowing that you can hire day boats from Wroxham Bridge, further upstream. Some have room for a buggy...

OS map
Explorer OL40

how far
4⁷⁄₁₀ miles

how long
3–4 hours

how easy

The majority of the path is on top of an embankment. This is firm, but can be grassy in places. The last stage is on a metalled track.

timberrr!

In Tudor times, the country around Upton and the nearby town of Acle was covered in dense oak forests whose trees were felled by the hundred to provide timber for Elizabeth I's warships. The name 'Acle' refers to a clearing in an oak forest, deriving from 'in the lea of the oaks'.

dad fact!

At the end of the dyke there is a rare windmill: Palmer's Hollow Post Mill. The post mill was the earliest design of windmill built in Europe, first appearing in England in the 12th century. The entire body of the mill could be spun around on a central pole, enabling the sails to catch the wind.

route

- From the car park at Upton Dyke, head past the boats and continue out along the left-hand bank of the watercourse.
- After ½ mile the dyke joins the main river – turn left and continue on the embankment path for 1½ miles, passing a windmill, on your left, along the way.
- When another river joins from the left, the path kinks naturally left along its bank. Follow this path for ½ mile, until you reach a metalled farm track on the left.
- Take this track and follow its zigzags back across country. When the road reaches the trees you should be able to see the boats of Upton Dyke on your left.
- A grassy path leads through some fields on your left, one of which is sometimes used as a camping spot by boat owners. This pops you back out at the main wharf, by the car park.
- You can also stay on the metalled road until it joins a country lane. Turn left and simply follow this road back to the car park.

getting there

From Norwich take the A47 east to Acle. Go through this town, heading north-west, towards Upton, which is signed. When you reach Upton, continue straight over the first junction, turn right at the next and then almost immediately left. This is Boat Dyke Road. At the end of this lane, turn right. After 200 metres, park under the trees near the boatyard, **OS grid ref. TG402128**.

rest and refresh

The White Horse pub at Upton is a historic inn with a family garden (01493 750696; www.whitehorseupton.co.uk).

further info

www.norfolkbroads.com

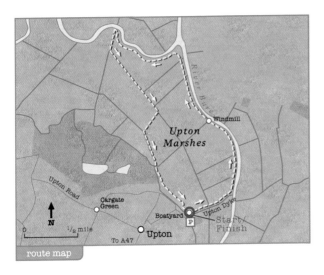

route map

blickling hall

From a far-flung corner of country estate, a leafy ramble leads you round its grounds in style. Field and forest edge onto manicured gardens and art galleries in this stately tour.

If ever there was a walk to make you dream of being an 18th-century aristocrat, this is it. At first you might feel like you're just on an ordinary outing in the country. On leaving the car parked in a forest glade you follow a plain track alongside open fields and beneath the boughs of aged oaks. The way turns left, and for a few pleasant moments you weave idly through woodland.

Then the trees suddenly cease, a clearing opens out before you and, to your left, you see something that will stop you in your tracks and change the whole tenor of the day.

It's a pyramid. Faced in grey stone and standing resolute beneath the swaying trees, it dominates this empty rectangle of Norfolk forest and demands closer inspection.

Erected in 1796 by Lady Caroline Suffield, it honours her father John Hobart, 2nd Earl of Buckinghamshire. The mausoleum is a heart-warming monument to love and reveals that you're in the once-private grounds of a fine property. You'll walk a full mile more before the house itself heaves into view, but what a sight; standing proudly amid the trees at the head of a glistening lake are the dramatic pinnacles, towers and chimneys of Blickling Hall.

The path ranges close to the formal gardens, with their 400-year-old yew hedges and historic trees, giving you a chance to enjoy their elegant architecture as the Hall's former occupants might have on returning from their morning ride. From here, you can choose to enter the grand Hall and explore its famous Long Gallery, which holds the National Trust's most important book collection (see dad fact!). Or you could re-energise with a Cromer crab and a glass of local ale at the nearby pub and let the young ones muck about in the adventure playground.

You can finish your fantasy of refinement by returning via the Grandstand Tower, built by the 2nd Earl for his guests to sit in finery and watch the horse racing. How splendid.

OS map
Explorer 252

how far
4 miles

how long
2½–3½ hours

how easy

Generally smooth going throughout on country lanes, forest paths and compacted track. One section over a grassy field.

most haunted

Blickling Hall was once voted the most haunted house in Britain in a National Trust survey. One celebrated spirit visitor is Anne Boleyn, who was born here. Her ghost is said to return home on 19 May every year, the anniversary of her execution. She arrives in a carriage driven by a headless coachman, and carries her own severed noggin neatly under one arm.

dad fact!

Blickling Hall's library is home to some of the most cherished manuscripts and books in England. A particularly important manuscript associated with the house is *The Blickling Homilies*, one of the earliest examples of its type of writing in English that still exists today.

route

- Follow the track from the car park south-east for 600 metres, with trees to the left and fields on the right.
- Turn left onto the compacted path through the woods. After crossing the mausoleum clearing, bear right and follow the path out of the trees, heading along a fence line towards a lone tree.
- Go on through a small wood and pick up the path signed 'Weavers' Way' until you reach the lake. Turn right and go along the nearside shore towards Blickling Hall, now visible in the distance.
- As you near the Hall, turn right to head along a grassy track and then left through a gate that leads to a road.
- Turn left, passing the pub on the right and play area on your left. The Hall is ahead, on the left.
- To return, take the small road opposite the pub and then bear left through a gate and along a wide track that heads through the estate towards the woods. This joins up with the path that you turned off to reach the mausoleum.

getting there

The car park is at a crook in the road, 1 mile south-east of Itteringham, **OS grid ref. TG162297**. From the A140, pass through Aylsham and head north-east to Blickling Hall on the minor road. Continue for 1¼ miles, past the Hall and Oulton Lodge. Take the next right, towards Itteringham, and then, after 400 metres, another right to Itteringham Common, where you should turn right. The car park is ¼ mile further on, on the right, where the road kinks sharply to the left.

rest and refresh

Blickling Hall has a café, loos and children's play area.
The Buckinghamshire Arms pub, just outside the main entrance to the Hall, has outdoor tables (01263 732133; www.bucksarms.co.uk).

further info

Blickling Hall: 01263 738030; www.nationaltrust.org.uk

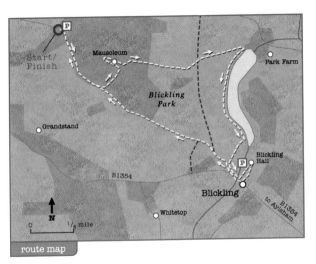

route map

overstrand to cromer

route

- From the car park at Overstrand, follow the obvious cliff-top path to the west. (Please keep to the right of way at the side of the golf course.)
- After passing the lighthouse, follow the path as it joins the road that passes in front of a row of houses.
- By the putting green, take the zigzag path to the beach. Turn back east along the beach.
- A narrow path in front of the huts will help you avoid having to traverse the soft sand.
- When this stops, head for the firm sand nearer the water. Depending on the tide, there might be a few groynes to negotiate, but these become few and far between.
- When you reach the concrete steps at Overstrand, take the sloping zigzag path up to the car park.

getting there

From Norwich, take the A140 (which becomes the A149) north to Cromer. At Cromer, take the minor road signposted to Overstrand. Turn left when you reach the town and park by the public loos at the cliff-top, **OS grid ref. TG247411**.

rest and refresh

It's easy to make a diversion into Cromer, which has lots of facilities, including loos and a café/bar on the pier (www.cromer-pier.com). There are also loos near the car park at Overstrand, and an ice cream van is usually here too.

further info

www.visitnorthnorfolk.com

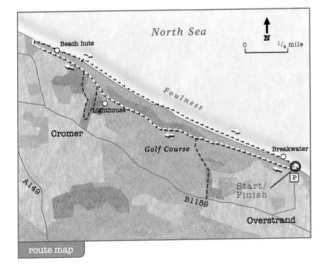

route map

cley marshes

A wetland rich in bird and wildlife is bounded by an awesome pebble strand and anchored by an ancient seaport. This is a seascape where the land battles wind, wave and water.

Raindrops pattern the still pools of water. A brisk salty breeze runs through your hair and reddens your cheeks. A tree, washed a pure white by the sea, poses nobly on the beach. Clouds speed above a windmill's ancient sails. And everywhere you go, the sweet chatter of birds fills the air.

It could only be Cley Marshes, a very different slice of England's coastline. You can see the individual elements of Cley's attractions elsewhere, but only here do they knit together into such a charismatic blanket of landscape.

Take the beach. As you walk out across the marsh, you have no suspicion it even exists. Then, suddenly, the land is replaced by a grand sweep of steeply banked pebbles, shelving into the deep as if a conjuror had made it vanish. Out to sea, the horizon forms a huge stage on which the weather plays out its dramas. And don't be surprised if you see a pair of inquisitive seal's eyes regarding you from between the waves. This is a beach that makes you want to sit down and write poems, not read Jackie Collins.

Then there's the nature reserve. The marshland may look rather plain, but the Norfolk Wildlife Trust has turned it into a fascinating place to visit. For a modest entrance fee, you walk out amid the reed beds on boardwalks to several well-positioned hides to get up close and personal with the wildlife. The track that brings you back from the beach runs amid an epic landscape of low-lying fields and shallow ponds dotted with wading birds. At the waterside, cattle graze contentedly beneath the fast-moving clouds.

Before long you'll find yourself pootling through the enticing thoroughfares of Cley-next-the-Sea. Town and ocean are no longer close, but remnants of their once-strong maritime marriage are visible in the café-crammed streets. Resist your hunger until you're back at the visitor centre, with its excellent café and viewing area. It's also eco-friendly, producing its own solar and wind energy. But more importantly, the chocolate cake is scrummy.

OS map
Explorer 251

how far
3½ miles

how long
2½–3½ hours

how easy

Mostly good going on tracks, paths or quiet roadsides. The path along the back of the beach is firm, with a short section of looser pebbles.

feathered friends

Cley Marshes nature reserve is the oldest of its kind in Britain, having been in the care of the Norfolk Wildlife Trust since 1926. It's an internationally important site for many rare breeding birds such as avocets, bearded tits, bitterns, marsh harriers and spoonbills. Visiting birds include brent geese, wigeons, pintails and many species of waders.

dad fact!

Cley was once one of England's busiest ports, but has not been next-the-Sea for nearly 400 years. Land reclamation pushed the coast outwards and caused the port to silt up. Many town buildings, including the windmill, used to line the quay. Echoes of the town's once-flourishing trade can be seen in the many Flemish gables on its buildings.

route

- From the car park at the visitor centre, cross the road and turn right, following the path that runs east.
- After 600 metres, turn left to walk along the signed track that heads out towards the banked beach in the distance.
- When you reach this beach, turn left along the narrow but firm path on the shoreward side of the shingle ridge.
- Follow this until you reach the car park at the end of the access road for Blakeney Point. There is an information board here.
- Turn left and head back inland, on the path that runs parallel with the road.
- When you reach the main road turn right to explore the village of Cley-next-the-Sea.
- To return to the start, turn left and take the footpath signposted 'NWT Cley Visitor Centre' that runs to the left of the main road.

getting there

The Cley Marshes visitor centre is on the A149 coast road (12 miles west of Cromer and 9 miles east of Wells-next-the-Sea) and is clearly signposted. Park here; **OS grid ref. TG053441**. You can also catch the Coasthopper (www.coasthopper.co.uk) bus service to the nature reserve from multiple towns along the Norfolk coast. There is a small charge to access the reserve – pay at the visitor centre.

rest and refresh

The visitor centre has an excellent café and there are several places for light bites in Cley, including the George Hotel, Cookes of Cley and the West Cottage café.
If you fancy picnicking on your walk, stock up at the Picnic Fayre delicatessen or Cley Smokehouse.

further info

www.cley.org.uk
www.norfolkwildlifetrust.org.uk

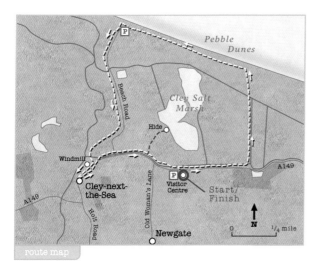

route map

central england

long compton

Church spires rise skywards from a nest of thatched roofs, and lush woods border patchwork fields. This secret circular walk reveals a crowd-free corner of the Cotswolds.

The golden-stone glories of Cotswold towns justly draw visitors to tramp their streets. Fine antique shops, ancient marketplaces, unexpected rivers, and the cottages – does anywhere do the English country cottage better than the Cotswolds? The thatched roofs, rich stone walls and flower-packed trellises framing oak doors and leaded windows... Picture-postcard photo opps await on every street corner.

But we think that the best place to appreciate a village around here is from far off, away from most of the visitors. Only from the top of a neighbouring hill can you see how the settlements sit within the landscape, following its curves and complementing its character.

The village of Long Compton snoozes between rounded hills like an old dog in a favourite armchair. So natural are the houses that they seem not so much to have been built, as to have formed underground and simply grown out of the earth into their current situation.

At least, that's what it looks like from the crest of the hill above Long Compton Woods. It certainly feels like a place that is properly lived in. The village is a working, breathing part of the landscape, not just a cluster of scenic holiday lets. The postman actually comes in for a cup of tea. Newspapers are read cover to cover on well-trimmed lawns. Every child in the village walks to school.

The world here is just so pleasant. Poppies embroider the borders of great fields of wheat. The quiet lanes are all butterflies and brambles. A sudden copse offers cool respite from the high summer sun. From an opening in the trees you can see that the next valley is just as lovely as the one behind you. And the one after that is too.

Perhaps when you arrive back in the village, you'll notice a thatcher replacing the roof of a house on the corner. It's slow work. The job looks like it's going to take him all summer. But that's fine, there's no rush. Not in these parts.

OS map
Explorer 191

how far
3⅕ miles

how long
2–2½ hours

how easy

Mostly good going on farm tracks, fieldside paths and minor roads. There is one kissing gate, which might be a squeeze depending on the size of your buggy.

roll with it

Near Long Compton are the Rollright Stones, a complex of megalithic monuments much talked about in local folklore, with many experts identifying them as the bodies of a king and his knights, petrified by a witch. Others say the stones were put there by Neolithic people, around 2,500 BC.

dad fact!

Nearby Chipping Campden is home to one of England's strangest festivals – the annual Cotswold Olympick Games. The event originated over 400 years ago to find the champions of sports including stick-fighting, wrestling, jumping in sacks, throwing the sledge hammer, dancing and even shin-kicking – which is still part of the Games today.

route

- At the north end of the village a minor road forks to the right, and just to the right of this a path is signposted leading into farmland to the east. (**OS grid ref. SP287333**.)
- Follow this as it weaves slowly along a hedgerow and then begins to gently climb.
- After ¼ mile it enters Long Compton Wood; 300 metres later, turn left up the track that leads to the minor country road.
- Turn right along this, for 100 metres, then turn left onto a track that heads through fields.
- After 400 metres you reach a house at the corner of some woods; turn left along the edge of the woods, walk for 500 metres, then turn left and head into another wood.
- Follow the path that weaves through the trees and pops you out on the country lane.
- Turn right and walk for 100 metres, then turn left through the kissing gate into the field that drops down the hillside.
- Long Compton is visible ahead of you. Take the path down the field's side and rejoin the track you took at the start.

getting there

Long Compton is on the A3400 from Oxford to Stratford-upon-Avon. From the M40, take the A422 and then the A361 to Banbury. A mile before Chipping Norton, turn right onto the A3400. Long Compton is 4 miles further on. Park where you can in the village. The walk starts at **OS grid ref. SP287333**.

rest and refresh

There are no facilities on the route itself.
The Red Lion pub in Long Compton has a nice outdoor space and also offers a children's menu (01608 684221; www.redlion-longcompton.co.uk).

further info

www.cotswolds.info

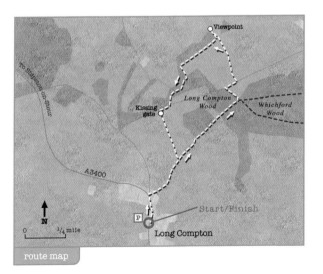

route map

sherborne park

The wide acres of Sherborne Park were once an aristocratic pleasure ground. They remain blissfully quiet today. On a brisk morning it'll just be you and the deer in the early mist.

'Be Outside, Be Alive!
Breathing in the air of nature
Seeing nature in its fullness of bloom,
Instead of listening to the humming of the refrigerator
Or seeing the untidy living room
Taking in the views with the naked eye
Feeling underfoot the crispness of the forest floor,
Instead of looking at the ironing pile growing higher
Or thinking about washing the kitchen floor...'

So begins C Paxton's paean, which could be the ethos of this book, but is actually one of many poems and artworks created by the adults and children of the local Rhymers' Club that you'll spy on this walk. Hidden in little woodland nooks on the rolling Sherborne Estate, they're there to make you stop a moment to think, smile and be charmed. And what a very good reason for being there that is.

This route is also charming: following fieldside tracks and ducking through a cool wood before trundling through the sleepiest of villages and returning amid more trees. Along the way, vistas of the curvy Cotswold Hills and winding Windrush Valley are ever-changing and delightful.

The oak, ash, beech and lime trees are stately and serene – keep an eye out for fallow and roe deer and an ear open for barn owls and woodpeckers. You'll also pass a circular seat built around an ancient tree – an irresistible picnic spot. In fact, the forest is full of treasures; tumbled logs and low trees that are perfect for clambering over and balancing on. There are even a few rope swings for older children to do their best Tarzan impersonations on.

If it's a warm day and you fancy cooling down after your walk, visit nearby Bourton-on-the-Water. It can be busy, but if your young ones are walking they will love dipping their toes in the shallow river that runs right through the main street of the village. And you'll enjoy it so much you might feel like writing a poem...

OS map
Explorer OL45

how far
3¹⁄₁₀ miles

how long
2–2½ hours

how easy

Gradients are easy and some of the route is on pavements; parts are on grassy woodland tracks and along field edges, which can be bobbly.

water wonderland
You can extend your walk by continuing to the water meadows that run from Sherborne village to the River Windrush. In the 18th century, farmers carefully landscaped these with channels and sluices to carry water from the river through the fields to improve winter grazing. Today they're home to otters, water voles and wading birds.

dad fact!
The estate was once part of the grounds of Sherborne House, originally a magnificent Elizabethan manor, then a Maharishi retreat, a boys' public school and now private apartments. The elegant ornamental pond there was actually dug by the schoolboys (under strict instruction, presumably) to be their unheated outdoor swimming pool.

route

- At Sherborne Estate's Ewe Pen Barn you can pick up a leaflet guide with maps of the various walks on the estate. Our route is the 'Family Fun Walk', coded purple.
- Exit the barn's car park and turn right, going east past the barn buildings on a track, and bear left where the path divides.
- At the edge of the field, turn left along the fence and continue into the wood.
- Follow the winding path through the trees, bearing left where it divides and you'll eventually reach a country lane.
- Turn right and follow the pavement past cottages and a view over Sherborne Brook.
- After ½ mile you reach Sherborne village. On the right is a gate by the phone box.
- Pass through this and go west along the edge of the field then south, beside the wood and then into the wood.
- Eventually you come out onto a fieldside track – turn right and you will pass a long beech avenue, which is worth exploring. Continue along the track, back to Ewe Pen Barn.

getting there

The walk starts at Ewe Pen Barn, which is just off the A40 between Burford and Northleach. Exit the M5 at junction 11, onto the A40. Turn left onto the minor road 3 miles east of Northleach and after 500 metres turn right at the sign for Ewe Pen Barn, where there is a car park at **OS grid ref. SP158143**.

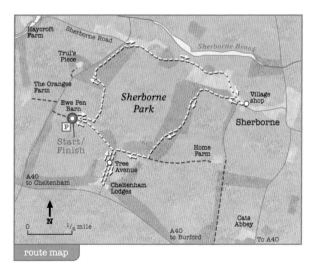

route map

rest and refresh

Sherborne village has a tea room and village shop.
There are also lots of fine cafés, tea rooms and pubs in Bourton-on-the-Water.

further info

www.nationaltrust.org.uk

cannop ponds

This lazy figure-of-eight walk loops around a favourite Forest of Dean beauty spot. It passes a popular pond-side picnic area on its way to quieter corners of the valley.

Cannop Ponds reflect the inner character of this forest like a pair of wise emerald eyes. Spend just a few minutes in this leafy bower and you'll feel your own senses sharpening to take in all the woodland delights. Reed warblers sing from the water's edge. Fishermen snooze on their wooden stations amid the rushes. Fallow deer nose their way softly through the trees. Waterfowl cruise up to say hello, ringed by the softest of ripples.

A wide path takes you away from the water on a carefree romp through the Cannop Valley's magnificent oak and pine woodland. This is a working forest, but the felling is done selectively and many of the trees you'll see here are several hundred years old. It's an ever-evolving landscape: one minute the trees are crowding in around you, the next a cutting clears a view.

As you roll through the forest breaks, the bracken and brambles run wild in a riotous hedgerow. Stands of spruce trees wait patiently like soldiers on parade. Beneath the woodland canopy insects drone by the bracken, bees zip from thistle to thistle and dragonflies dance above reeds.

After touring the forest, our route loops back to the ponds along a wide cycleway. An elegant arched bridge leads you over the rippling little river that links the two lakes. The path then dives into the coolness of the trees on the far bank of the upper pond. To your right, the water is patterned by lilies, while ahead, the path finds a way through the marshy nature reserve's tall reeds and soon you're enjoying the final delights of the walk: a switchback stretch through glades and dells that are simply crying out to have dens built in them.

It's strange to think that the area owes its existence to industry. The ponds were created in the 1820s to supply water for a nearby ironworks. And the wonderful wide cycleway that runs through the valley floor was once a mineral railway. Progress can be a beautiful thing.

OS map
Explorer OL14

how far
2¾ miles

how long
1¾–2½ hours

how easy

The going is mostly very easy on surfaced paths, but there are a few rooty bits in the woods.

the historic forest

The Norman kings once galloped here on their hunts, but today it's a peaceful haven for humans and animals. Fallow deer still graze amid the trees. In Tudor times the wood's mighty oaks helped build Britain's navy. The Spanish Armada was instructed to destroy the forest should its invasion of England succeed. The Forest of Dean became England's first national forest park in 1938.

dad fact!

For more than 700 years the Freeminers have dug coal from beneath the Forest of Dean. In 1296, Edward I decreed that men born in the Hundred of St Briavels had the right to mine coal, apparently as a reward for their help in recapturing Berwick-upon-Tweed from the Scots. There are still around 150 Freeminers today, working two full-time mines.

route

- From the car park, walk along the easy tarmac road into the woods.
- When you reach the picnic area by the ponds, look out for the red-marked post. (From here on, much of this route is marked as the 'Cannop Ponds Trail', but the posts are somewhat erratic.)
- Head left on this winding path through the trees. When you reach a wider track, turn right and continue straight along the forest break for ¼ mile, until you reach an angled track turning right.
- Take this and continue along it until you meet a cycleway, then turn right.
- This takes you back to the picnic area; here turn left, over the arched bridge and follow the path round the far side of the top pond.
- Turn right when you reach a wooden bridge and follow the path between hedgerows and then through the wood.
- This brings you back to the tarmac road; turn left to head back to your car.

getting there

From Gloucester, take the A40 heading west. Just after Huntley, turn left onto the A4136 and continue, through Mitcheldean, towards Coleford. One mile after Brierley, turn left onto the B4234 and continue for 2 miles; turn left at the junction with the B4226 and after 100 metres turn right at the signed entry to Cannop Ponds. Park before the barrier; **OS grid ref. SO610116.**

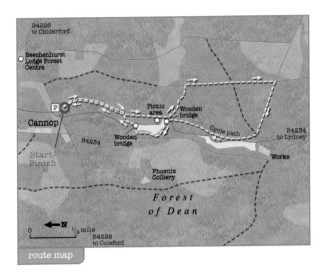

route map

rest and refresh

There are no loos or permanent refreshment facilities; usually on summer weekdays there is a mobile snack van, but it's best to bring a picnic.

further info

www.forestry.gov.uk

symonds yat

The level banks of the River Wye make for a soothing walk along its deep, treelined gorge, while a low-slung suspension bridge and an ancient ferry add the perfect amount of fun.

Deep in a steep wooded gorge sits the village of Symonds Yat, cleaved in two by the River Wye. This is the heart of an area of outstanding natural beauty and most visitors head for the honeypot pubs and cafés to soak up the views. But trundle off along the riverside and you enter a quieter world of leafy paths and sun-drenched picnic spots, all graced by the meandering might of the river itself.

This woodland realm certainly deserves its AONB status: aged broadleaf trees flank the slopes, and riverside glades form perfect playgrounds for butterflies as well as toddlers. Bring your binoculars, too – the rocky outcrops that rear out of the trees are beloved by many raptors. From here they survey the wooded walls of their domain, waiting for an unsuspecting lunch to scurry by. Keep your eyes on the skies and you may very well see buzzards, goshawks and hobbies as well as a majestic pair of peregrine falcons that nest annually within sight of Symonds Yat Rock.

The turning point of the walk is at Biblins campsite, where a pedestrian suspension bridge that looks like it should be in a Himalayan gorge spans the river. Happily, a buggy fits perfectly on its boards. Not many people know that, as well as the river, this bridge crosses a national border. A quirk of geography means that shortly before you reach the bridge on the eastern side of the river, you cross into Wales. You then return to England at the midpoint of the bridge. Canoeists and rafters drift under your feet, laughing and splashing in the twisting current.

The return journey on the other bank feels more remote. The good track winds in and out of the trees, passing some ancient mill workings, now tumbledown and moss-covered. The walk has a very special ending – a boat trip on one of the last hand-pulled cable ferries in the world. Remember to bring some change to pay the hard-working ferryman. As you step out of the boat you'll thoroughly deserve a spot of refreshment in one of the many welcoming pubs and cafés that you passed at the start.

OS map
Explorer OL14

how far
3 miles

how long
1¾–2½ hours

how easy

Mostly very easy going; some stony bits on the west bank track.

cat's cave

Over the millennia the elements have gouged many caves out of the sheer limestone cliffs in the River Wye gorge. In one of them, 'King Arthur's cave', archaeologists have discovered the remains of a hyena family as well as sabre-toothed cat bones.

dad fact!

The village's odd name comes from a 17th-century sheriff, Robert Symonds, and a local word for 'gate'. But its history stretches back much further. Perched 152 metres above the river is the spectacular viewpoint of Symonds Yat Rock, where Iron Age man built a fort around 2,000 years ago.

route

- From the car park, walk past the Royal Lodge Hotel and along the good track through the trees.
- Follow this for 1¼ miles, as it curves with the river.
- Cross at Biblins suspension bridge, then return along the path on the opposite bank.
- This path rises as you approach the houses of Symonds Yat West.
- When you reach the zigzag road you need to walk down to the right to reach the cable ferry that will transport you back to your starting point.

getting there

From Gloucester, take the A40 heading west. Just after Huntley, turn left onto the A4136 and continue through Mitcheldean towards Coleford. At Five Acres, turn right, onto the B4432 and follow signs for Symonds Yat, which is 3 miles further on. When you reach the bottom of the hill by the river, take a sharp left and park near the Royal Lodge Hotel, **OS grid ref. SO562158**.

rest and refresh

The garden of the Royal Lodge Hotel is a lovely spot to sit with your family (01600 890238; www.royalhotel-symondsyat.com). The Saracens Head Inn, situated right by the ferry, also has an outside terrace (01600 890435; saracensheadinn.co.uk).

further info

www.royalforestofdean.info

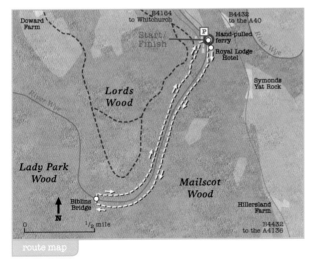

route map

stratford riverbank

To buggy, or not to buggy, that is the question. Well, when the route is as unforgettable as this, you buggy. Roll along a river out into the country, on a path that is pure poetry.

The park by Stratford-Upon-Avon's riverside appears perfectly ordinary at first – a lovely flat stretch of grass, with swans and rowing boats in the water and a place to buy ice cream nearby. But the further along the river you walk, the more special this ramble becomes.

Little ferries tootle over the river, taking the thirsty to quintessentially English pubs. There are lots of spots under the willow trees to spread out your tartan rug and flop down. You'll spy a spire rising elegantly from the treeline on the far bank; its church has a wonderful secret awaiting discovery on the walk's homeward leg, but for now its slender beauty is enough to captivate.

A little further on, a pair of severe-looking herons have set up a checkpoint at a cascading weir, while a colourful boat eases into a lock and all hands scurry into action. There's so much to see that before you know it you're out in the countryside. Where did Stratford go? Who cares? Just keep on rolling – there's more to discover yet.

Eventually you cross the river and return along the hem of patchwork fields towards town, where you visit that lovely church, approached via an avenue of lime trees. There's a tranquillity in the air here that can only come from eight centuries of devotion. And inside, there's something even more special. This is Holy Trinity Parish Church, where William Shakespeare was baptised and laid to rest. It's very touching to see the plain stone with verse inscription that marks his grave. It remembers a man who achieved more in his field than anyone else ever has or will, who met with royalty and became rich; but who never forgot the land of his boyhood. It was to Stratford that Shakespeare retired, and it was here that he died.

You can see fascinating entries in the record books from all those centuries ago. Charmingly, the church also has a selection of Elizabethan dressing-up clothes; so older kids can have a bit of fun as you pay your respects to the bard.

OS map
Explorer 205

how far
route a: 3⅘ miles
route b: 2¹⁄₁₀ miles

how long
route a: 2½–3½ hours
route b: 1½–2 hours

how easy
route a   route b

Both routes have a few steps over a footbridge. **Route a** has a further set of steps up and a set down. It's a bit of a puff, but it's over quickly, and it adds a wonderful rural section to the walk.

playtime

At the Royal Shakespeare Theatre older kids can follow the clues on the free Treasure Trail to learn about the theatre's history. There is also a fun Play Cart that comes out into the café with books, costumes and art stuff to help children discover Shakespeare.

dad fact!

Shakespeare died on 23 April 1616 – his birthday. In his will he made a point of leaving his wife Anne, 'my second best bed'. No one is sure if this was an insult or he was thoughtfully ensuring she got the more meaningful matrimonial bed.

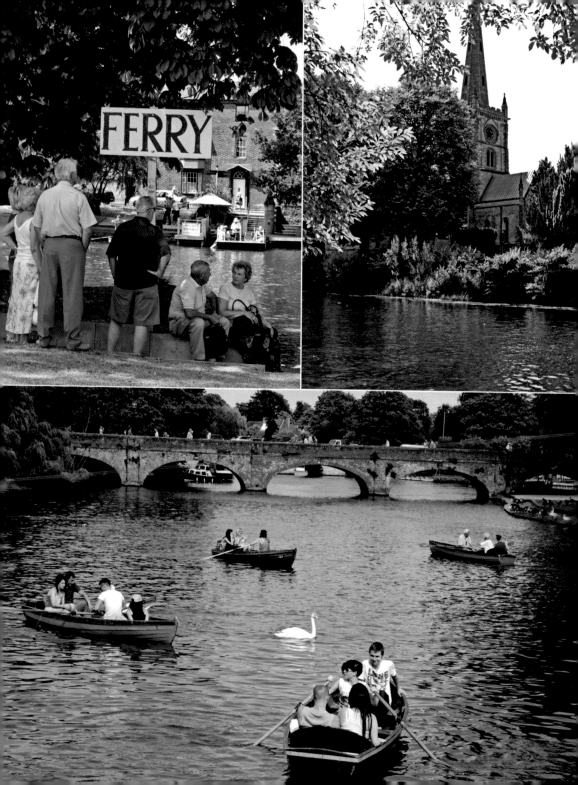

route a

- From the recreation ground, turn left along the river.
- Pass a lock and weirs, then a footbridge and a road bridge.
- 300 metres after the road bridge you reach another lock and weir. Take the path up the slope into the trees. There are steps up, and then down, in the wood. The path leaves the wood and skirts fields until it reaches an old rail line.
- Turn right onto this, cross the river, then immediately leave the old rail line to the right and return to the riverside path.
- Follow the path along field edges back towards town.
- The path leaves the river (after the road bridge) and goes along Mill Lane. Follow it to Holy Trinity Parish Church.
- Pass through its grounds and take the obvious riverside route back to town, going over the bridge in front of the Royal Shakespeare Theatre back to the starting point.

route b

- For a shorter walk, start on **route a** but turn around at the second weir, then cross the river at the footbridge just after the road bridge (a few steps up and down).
- Follow the directions towards the end of **route a** from where it leaves the river and goes along Mill Lane.

getting there

Head for the recreation ground in Stratford-Upon-Avon's town centre. The cricket club just behind the recreation ground also has some pay and display spots, **OS grid ref. SP205547**.

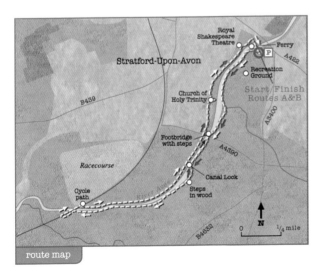

route map

rest and refresh

The Royal Shakespeare Theatre is buggy-friendly and has a restaurant and café (www.rsc.org.uk).
There are also various snack shacks at the riverside.
The recreation ground has a playground, paddling pool and public loos.

further info

www.stratford-upon-avon.co.uk

ellesmere

Pass through a historic market town, ease along towpaths and past the placid meres of 'Shropshire's Lake District'. It's an easy amble but with a surprise, so take a torch...

You can spend a memorable afternoon at Ellesmere simply by parking at the visitor centre on the treelined lake shore, buying some grain to feed the swans, enjoying an ice cream and then strolling into town for a nice cuppa.

But there's a lot more to Ellesmere than that. To start with, the placid pool by the visitor centre is one of nine such meres in the area. There's also the ancient market town itself, with its gardens, lashings of coffee shops and a particularly fine pub or two. Then there's the picturesque Llangollen Canal, looping round the back of the town, which has a marina, colourful barges, buggy-friendly towpaths and, best of all, a spooky tunnel.

It was the ancient Britons who first strolled with their babes here. They set up camp by the water's edge to fish, trade and just potter about the meres. Modern Britons do much the same. The Mere's visitor centre is a honeypot for young and old. You pass along its edge, knee-deep in honking geese, and then walk through quieter waterside gardens – perfect for avoiding the beaked peckpockets.

Visit on a Tuesday and you can browse in Ellesmere's weekly market, which was founded way back in 1221. There are also lots of shops selling cake-based nutrition. A constitutional walk along the towpath then brings you to Ellesmere Tunnel. You can avoid this by going over the top, but only scaredy-cats would do that. The path is narrow, but has a safety railing all the way. The echoes are tremendous, so prep your best ghostly voice and go for it.

Emerging at the other end, the path you're on becomes a kind of raised causeway between the canal and another limpid lake. This is Blake Mere, apparently created by the melting of vast lumps of ice some 10,000 years ago.

For yet more watery fun, check the times of the *Lady Katherine* steamer at the visitor centre. A cruise on the Mere makes a fitting end to a wonderful day's walking.

OS map
Explorer 240

how far
4¹/₁₀ miles

how long
2½–3 hours

how easy

Easy going on towpaths, streets and paths. One short section is on a grassy path through a field.

telford's triumph
Thomas Telford lived in Ellesmere from 1793 to oversee the building of what is now the Llangollen Canal. Featuring spectacular viaducts, bridges and tunnels, this prodigious feat of engineering has been partly designated a UNESCO World Heritage site and is very much worth a visit.

dad fact!
You might notice that the bowling green you pass towards the end of the walk has a particularly commanding position above the Mere – this is no accident. The green here was originally the motte of long-gone Ellesmere Castle, which was an 11th-century motte-and-bailey fortification.

route

- From the car park, walk back to the road and turn right, passing the Mere and bearing right to head along the water's edge to Cremorne Gardens.
- Go through the gate and continue into the gardens, then take the first path on the left, towards the town centre.
- At the road turn right, cross over and turn left down Watergate Street.
- Turn right at the signpost for Canal Wharf and then left at a T-junction, passing the Spar.
- Turn left down Wharf Road, and on to the Llangollen Canal.
- Take the towpath, cross the canal over the bridge, pass the marina and continue to, and through, the Ellesmere Tunnel.
- The towpath opens out and Blake Mere appears on your left. At the end of the lake is a picnic table – snack time!
- Go back through the tunnel and along the towpath. (Or walk up to the road at the tunnel for a shortcut back to your car.)
- Four hundred metres before the marina, a path goes right; follow this into a wood and out onto a lane.
- Turn left and go past the bowling green, then bear right and go through the field that slopes down to the Mere.
- Return, past the visitor centre, to your car.

getting there

Ellesmere is on the A495, where it meets the A528 between Oswestry and Whitchurch. Park near the visitor centre by the Mere (for a fee), **OS grid ref. SJ408343**.

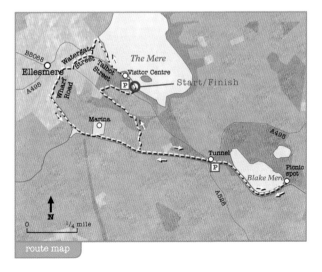

rest and refresh

The Boathouse visitor centre at the Mere has recently been refurbished and has a lovely café with a terrace and modern loos.
You'll also find several good cafés in Ellesmere town, including the Talgarth Tearooms (01691 624440; www.talgarthtearooms.co.uk).

further info

Visitor centre: 01691 622981
www.shropshire.gov.uk

tissington
and dovedale

Two equally alluring walks in the Derbyshire Dales make a day to remember: a smooth stroll through farmland to a typical English village, then an amble to a wild little dale.

Wheeshing bursts of steam, trilling whistles and buzzing crowds would have made Tissington station a throbbing hive of humanity 50 years ago. Many visitors started their exploration of the Peak District from here, arriving on specially chartered excursion trains.

It's more peaceful now that the railway has gone, but Tissington is still a centre for explorers. The track bed was one of the first old lines to be turned into a public path for walkers, cyclists and riders – the Tissington Trail – and this easy-going route starts you on a special rural journey.

You'll roll through clearings lushly lined with ash, beech and young oak trees as banks of wild flowers line the hayfields. Then the track rises and you emerge on the edge of an undulating dale, where the hillside tumbles away before you in a panorama of green fields, stone walls, neat copses and, in the distance, crumpled peaks of higher hills.

You could wander along this line for miles yet, but today our little loop returns across the quiet fields and into Tissington itself, easily one of the most picturesque villages in England. The whole hamlet is part of a single estate, which has been cared for by the FitzHerbert family since Richard III was in short trousers. Happily, inappropriate development has never been part of the dynasty's plans. The 40 cottages and 13 farms remain unspoiled and the village centre, with its Norman church, historic wells, green and duck pond, is a picture of peace and harmony. There are also some very nice shops.

While you're here, you really ought to spend even an hour or two exploring nearby Dovedale. Just a five-minute tootle from Tissington, this starts as a pretty river valley and then swiftly changes into a dramatic limestone ravine, with sheer, tree-clad slopes and riotous wild flowers. There is also an irresistible set of stepping stones (yes, you will get the buggy across). The dale is buggyable for nearly two miles and makes a very serene spot for a picnic.

OS map
Explorer OL24

how far
route a: 6 miles; **route b:** 3 miles; **route c:** 1½ miles

how long
route a: 3½–4½ hours; **route b:** 2–2½ hours; **route c:** 1–1¼ hours

how easy
all routes

Mostly excellent going on all routes. A slightly rough fieldside section on **routes a** and **b**; some rocky sections on **route c** and an optional set of stepping stones.

well dressed
An ancient Derbyshire tradition comes to Tissington each May – Well Dressing. The six village wells are decorated with flowers and Bible-themed pictures in time for Ascension Day. People pack the streets to enjoy the riot of colour and entertainment. The tradition dates from 1348, when villagers thanked the wells for their escape from the Black Death.

dad fact!
The River Dove is a famed trout stream and it was a favourite haunt of Izaak Walton, 17th-century author of *The Compleat Angler*, a celebration of the art and sport of fishing.

route a

- From the car park in Thorpe, go east to access the Tissington Trail and turn left onto it.
- Follow the trail for 2 miles, passing Tissington station. At **OS grid ref. SK172537** turn left and head south-west then south through several fields before joining the road that leads into Tissington village, follow it through the village.
- At the old station rejoin the trail and return to Thorpe.

route b

- Begin at Tissington station, following **route a**'s village loop.

route c

- From the National Trust Dovedale car park, start up the road into the dale then cross the river and take the path that runs along the right-hand bank.
- Continue along the dale to the large flight of steps.
- Return, taking the optional route across the stepping stones and back down the road if you wish.

getting there

route a: From the A515, Ashbourne to Buxton road, follow signs for Thorpe and park in the village at **OS grid ref. SK164505**.
route b: From the A515, follow signs for Tissington village; taking the minor road into the village, passing the pond on your right. Park at Tissington station car park, **OS grid ref. SK178522**.
route c: Go through Thorpe and follow the winding road signed 'Dovedale'. After ⅛ mile you cross a river; take the next right and continue to the National Trust car park, **OS grid ref. SK146509**.

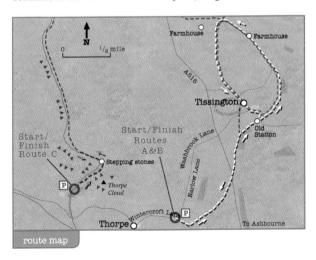

route map

rest and refresh

The nearby Bluebell Inn (on the A515, ½ mile from Tissington) has a garden with play area, swings and a pets' paddock. Little ones are also allowed in the bar, which has a children's menu (01335 350317; www.bluebelltissington.co.uk). The Old Coach House Tea Rooms in Tissington village offer fine lunches and afternoon teas and have outdoor space (01335 350501). There's also a tea room at Bassett Wood Farm (¾ mile from the village), where youngsters can watch the cows go by as you enjoy a cuppa (01335 350254).

further info

www.derbyshireuk.net

wild moor

This airy tour above Buxton delivers Peak District views without the puffing. Enter a rare and remote stretch of country: the high, wild moorland where rivers are born.

The lofty, rough moors of the Peak District might not seem like good buggying country, but we're about to let you in on a secret. Just a few miles outside Buxton there's a car park by a crook in the road where you'll find a little pond and some splendid views. There's also an oddly flat and grassy path that curves into the heart of the high moor.

What's this path doing perched up on this hillside? It's actually the track bed of an old railway, originally built to transport mineral ore. Follow its elegant curves and the deeper you get into the hills, the more you realise that it's Mother Nature who wears the trousers here. Our ancestors may have extended civilisation's reach with the railway, but it was a spindly lifeline. When the winter clouds scoured the hilltops it must have been brutally tough for the men who worked these quarries.

The railway relinquished its hold long ago, and now the natural elements rule this world again. At first the path is so easy that you'll be able to switch off and let your senses soak up your surroundings. As you round a bend, you'll see a hidden ravine opening up, its snaking streambed awash with fragrant wild flowers. On the far side of Goyt's Moss, the muscular flanks of Shining Tor dominate the horizon. The hillside below you is a subtle masterwork of interwoven grasses and heathers. Skylarks rise suddenly from the ground and burst into song.

Eventually the track bed ends at a bricked-up tunnel. From here the route cascades down the valley, on a more eventful path that'll do wonders for your abs. But before you roll down the slopes, open the door in the tunnel face. An echoing, dripping emptiness leads into the heart of the hillside. It's tempting but shiver-inducing to step inside.

Afterwards you can leave these airy hillsides and return to civilisation in Buxton. The Pavilion Gardens have flowerbeds, fountains and a miniature train. It's lovely, really. But it's just not the same as the high, wild moor.

OS map
Explorer OL24

how far
3⅕ miles

how long
2–2½ hours

how easy

The going at first is very easy; the downhill section has a few bumps and steps. The last push to the car park is steep.

bubbling buxton

Buxton is the highest market town in England, standing at 305 metres above sea level. In the 18th century, it was developed as a spa resort, thanks to its natural geothermal spring, which still rises in the town centre at a constant 28°C. You can fill your water bottles at St Ann's Well near the town's famous Crescent.

dad fact!

Much of the walk is along the old Cromford and High Peak Railway. This was completed in 1832 and was one of England's steepest and highest lines. Its summit at Ladmanlow was 385 metres above sea level, which compares with the present day highest summit of 356 metres at Ais Gill on the Settle to Carlisle line.

route

- From the car park, walk past the pond and take the obvious wide path that runs towards the south east.
- Follow this for a mile, until you reach the blocked-up railway tunnel.
- Take the path on the right that drops down the hillside.
- Cross the brook and continue on the path as it goes down the valley's side.
- The path reaches a wider track that passes by a wood, and rounds the hillside to give views of Errwood Reservoir.
- Follow the track as it cuts back on itself and climbs steeply up the hillside to the start.

getting there

From Buxton, take the A5004 towards Whaley Bridge. After 2 miles take the minor road on the left, Goyt's Lane, that leads down to Errwood Reservoir. After ¼ mile, park on the left just before the little pond, **OS grid ref. SK024753**.

rest and refresh

There are no facilities on the route. The New Pavilion Café in the Pavilion Gardens in Buxton is a fine family-friendly spot, with a children's menu and local products on offer (01298 23114; www.paviliongardens.co.uk).

further info

www.visitbuxton.co.uk

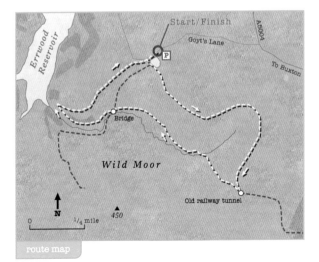

route map

north west

derwentwater

Listen to the lapping of the waves and the sighing of the trees on an oak-shrouded lake shore. Your heart will soar over the circling hills and you'll feel miles from anywhere.

Derwentwater is deservedly popular. Its enticing waters are guarded by a huddle of wooded fells, while the lively town of Keswick nestles on its northern shore. This can be a busy place in the height of summer, but many visitors don't realise that it's easy to escape the crowds and stroll along wide paths in a waterside forest.

Simply take one of the Keswick Launches that spin constantly round a seven-point circuit of the lake, and disembark 10 breezy minutes later at Hawse End. When the bubbling swish of the boat's engine dies away, you'll find yourself happily stranded on Derwentwater's wilder western shoreline.

The walk from here is simple: head south along the lakeside. But you'll discover plenty of treasures in Brandelhow Wood to enrich your afternoon... Pebbly bays washed by little waves under the drooping fringes of oak trees. Sudden sculptures proudly tenanted by squirrels. Sun-dappled patches of grass just begging to be picnicked on. While above and beyond it all runs a high collar of rolling hills: Bleaberry Fell and Walla Crag form a rugged backdrop over the water; Catbells and High Spy rise steeply at your back.

You can turn around at any point in the walk or pick up a ferry from one of the Brandelhow jetties. Times are posted on boards by each jetty. But if your wheels are rolling smoothly it's worth wandering on into the glorious mixed woodland of Manesty Park.

When you finally decide to return to the bustle of the town, do take a moment to lead your family out onto the little wooden landing pier and just have a sit. Quite often there are parties of school children out adventuring on the water in canoes, dinghies or even Viking longboats. The pirate shouts and laughter of the would-be Swallows and Amazons are infectious, and will send you skimming back over the waves with a smile on your face.

OS map
Explorer OL4

how far
4⅕ miles

how long
3–4 hours there and back; 10 minutes each way on the ferry.

how easy

The path is mostly wide with a compacted stone surface. There are occasional rooty bits in the woodland.

pencils ready?
Keswick farmers had long used local deposits of graphite to mark their sheep, and in 1832 the UK's first pencil factory was built here. The industry still thrives and there is a fascinating Pencil Museum in town – it's an inspiring place to take artistic youngsters if the weather turns really wet.

dad fact!
Derwentwater is the last remaining native habitat of the vendace – a freshwater whitefish that has only ever been found at four sites in Britain. The other three locations were Bassenthwaite Lake (also in Cumbria) and Scotland's Castle and Mill Lochs in Lochmaben, but sadly the fish is now extinct in all three.

route

- From the Hawse End jetty, head west until you reach the signposted track that passes below the Hawse End Outdoor Centre buildings.
- Follow the signpost for the lakeshore leading off the tarmac and through a wide gate.
- Continue south along this route as it weaves through the woodland.
- After passing the High Brandelhow jetty, the path joins a metalled track into Manesty Park.
- Turn here and retrace your steps.

getting there

Keswick is on the A66, and is signposted from the M6. Leave your car at one of the parking areas in town. Take a Keswick Launch from the Keswick boat landings to Hawse End jetty, **OS grid ref. NY251213**. Alternatively, drive to Hawse End from Keswick on a minor road. There are some parking spots near Hawse End at **OS grid ref. NY247212**; in summer there is also usually an enterprising lad who will let you park in his dad's field for a small sum.

rest and refresh

None en route, but there are plenty of good places to grab a bite in Keswick including the Lakeland Pedlar, a wholefood café with outside tables and a children's menu (01768 774492; www.lakelandpedlar.co.uk). There is an excellent market on Saturdays.

Public loos can be found near the central car park in Keswick.

further info

www.keswick-launch.co.uk
www.keswick.org

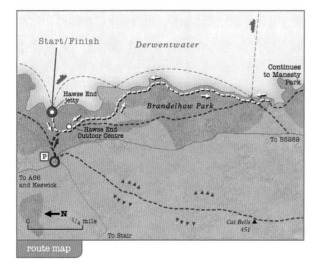

route map

blea tarn

Save this simple saunter round a high lake for a fine day and the rolling mountain views will reward you with the most tranquil spot for walking you're ever likely to enjoy.

It's no fun getting into your car at 4.15am and driving randomly around the streets trying to soothe some peace into a wide-awake baby. But if you're staying near Langdale when your blue-eyed alarm goes off at daft o'clock, you might find matters a little different. Because then you can whizz Junior up the winding little road to Blea Tarn.

Here you can pace slowly together round a beautiful blue bowl of water, cradled in the arms of the surrounding mountains. You'll have the place all to yourselves (if you don't count the birds, squirrels and deer) and, when you've chosen the perfect carved wooden bench, you can simply sit for an hour or so and watch the sun rise over the roof of England. Even if it doesn't send your baby back to sleep, it will certainly give you a wonderful sense of peace and an unforgettable start to the day.

Blea Tarn is just as gorgeous at other times, of course. Perched 200 metres above sea level on a knobbly ridge that separates the valleys of Great and Little Langdale, it offers a lofty view of some of the highest and most rugged peaks in the country. And on a still day, Blea's reflective waters will double your viewing pleasure with a perfect reflection of the famous Langdale Pikes.

The tarn itself is small, but the surrounding landscape is on an epic scale and your imagination can wander for miles. The little twists in the path will delight drifting eyes with a sudden flash of previously hidden forest or the mercury vein of a little brook. One of these streams has a pebbly ford as well as a wooden bridge – perfect for a spot of wellie-splashing.

If you visit in spring or summer you'll pass patches of grass given an Impressionist splash of colour by wild alpine flowers. Come on a sunny day and you'll see why the tarn is named after an ancient local word for dark blue; the water becomes a shining sapphire, cleaved and laid flat to dazzle happy passers-by.

OS map
Explorer OL6

how far
2 miles

how long
1½–2 hours

how easy

The route is suitable for all buggies to the end of the lake shore. The continuation to the head of the valley is a little rougher.

a 19th-century spaghetti junction

Below Blea Tarn is the quiet valley of Little Langdale. Although peaceful today, 200 years ago this was one of the busiest parts of the Lake District. It formed a major intersection of old pack-horse routes, with roads from Ravenglass in the west, Keswick in the north, Ambleside in the east and Coniston in the south all crossing here. The vale would have been alive with large numbers of men and animals, all travelling to market.

dad fact!

Blea Tarn will relax you, but excite scientists: it was gouged out by huge ice sheets and the sediments in its shallow basin offer a near perfect glimpse of the ecological ages between then and now.

route

- The path starts directly opposite the National Trust Blea Tarn car park and runs in a simple arc round the southern then western edge of the tarn.
- Most people turn back where the path leaves the woodland (**OS grid ref. NY292045**) but, if your buggy can manage a rougher track, you can enjoy a further ¼ mile of lovely views as the track continues to near the head of the little valley.

getting there

Take the unclassified road that links the western ends of Great and Little Langdale. This is narrow, steep and twisty; please drive carefully. Park at the National Trust pay and display area opposite the tarn, **OS grid ref. NY295043**.

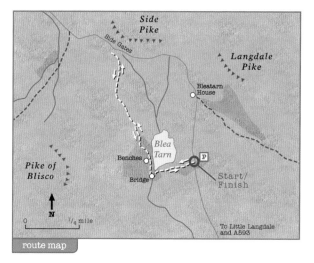

route map

great langdale beck

This chameleon walk weaves from riverbank, through lakeside meadow, into woodland and over roaring waterfalls. To top it off, fine local food and drink await at either end...

This walk is like one of the Cumbrian characters you might get chatting to over an ale on a winter's night: plain and pleasant at first glance but with subtler depths that only reveal themselves after lengthier acquaintance.

First introductions are modest: you pass the inviting Britannia Inn and bowling green at Elterwater to join the level track into the trees by Great Langdale Beck. As the glassy water chatters companionably beside you, it seems like a simple saunter is all that's in store today. But the winding path will playfully change its character several times over the next few hours, rewarding the wanderer with new surroundings and unexpected views.

No sooner have you stopped looking for fish among the grey stones of the riverbed than a little wood has hidden the water from you, and your spotter's eyes drift upwards to see who's twittering in the treetops. Then you pass another gate and suddenly the wood is gone – the world around you opening out wide into a water meadow with glorious views of the frowning Langdale Pikes. It's the perfect place to rest for a moment and watch the ripples toy with the reflections of trees and hills.

After a few slow minutes amid the sheep and ducks, the river gets restless. On reaching a forested outcrop it hurls itself through a series of jagged rocks to become a roaring, crashing brute – or Skelwith Force, as it's formally known. A few mossy twists under the trees and the path pops you out at the village of Skelwith Bridge. Cafés abound at this popular watering hole, but the smooth stepped rocks by the river simply beg you to join them for a bite outdoors.

The homeward path takes on one final guise – the bustling yard of a slate works. Here the stone from a nearby quarry is cut and polished to exquisite perfection. Quite a few fascinated youngsters will leave with a new nameplate for their bedroom door: a lasting reminder of the real character of Langdale.

OS map
Explorer OL7

how far
3⅔ miles

how long
2–3 hours

how easy

Mostly easy going on a level compacted surface; slightly bumpier and hillier in the woods at Skelwith Bridge; a short section on the road.

pikes and pints
Dominating Great Langdale are the Langdale Pikes, a group of dizzying peaks on the northern side of the dale. At their foot stands the characterful Old Dungeon Ghyll pub. Owned by the National Trust, the 'ODG' is famous for its Hikers Bar, where many a climber has supped after a long day on the hills.

dad fact!
Stone has been worked in Great Langdale for millennia. During the Neolithic period the locals excelled at making stone axes, with their workmanship being found right across the British Isles. Slate production boomed following the Elizabethan period, and there are still a few working quarries.

route

- Take the gate at the end of the car park to the wide stone path that runs alongside Great Langdale Beck.
- The track continues through a wood and along the shores of Elterwater.
- At the end of the meadow, pass through a gate and turn right over Woodburn Bridge.
- Follow the path through the wood and turn left at the road, continuing for 200 metres into Skelwith Bridge.
- Pause here for refreshments if you wish, before following the signposted path through the slate works and making a close approach to Skelwith Force.
- You will rejoin the path that brought you to the bridge over the river, from where you retrace your steps back to Elterwater.

getting there

Take the A593 from Ambleside or Coniston and turn at Skelwith Bridge onto the B5343, continuing for 1¼ miles to the signposted left turn into Elterwater. Langdale Rambler bus no. 516 runs between Ambleside and Elterwater from March to October. Start this walk from Elterwater's National Trust car park, **OS grid ref. NY328048.**

rest and refresh

There are public loos at Elterwater and refreshments at the welcoming Britannia Inn (01539 437210; britinn.net), Elterwater, and Chesters Café (01539 434711; www.chestersbytheriver.co.uk), Skelwith Bridge.

further info

www.visitcumbria.com

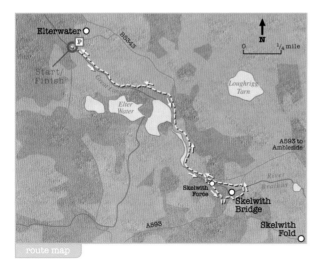

route map

tarn hows

In the hills behind Beatrix Potter heartland lie the sleepy waters of Tarn Hows. Here you can roll round the lakes on a perfect path, overlooking hills, dale, forests and moor.

The circuit of Tarn Hows deservedly draws many visitors on summer days, but if you come here on a drowsy evening once the crowds have hurried back to Hawkshead, you will be rewarded with a memorable amble around a serene lake.

Your first view of the tarn is from the top of a grassy hill. This flattish viewpoint offers a perfect picnic spot, but it's the one chosen by people who won't explore any further. Better to trundle on along the easy-going path and see if you can find your own little nook among the trees.

After dropping down to lake level, the path rollercoasters through the forest, twisting as it goes, to throw open unexpected snapshots of beauty. The scenery is stunning and there are plenty of benches and rest places from which to take it all in.

At the far side of the tarn, marking the start of the return leg, is a neat little bridge. This is a good spot to let any older kids burn off some energy – a stile nearby leads to a path up a knobbly hill that offers more fine views of some of the area's highest peaks: Wetherlam in the Coniston Fells, the Helvellyn range and the Langdale Pikes. Meanwhile you can sit with any younger ones and cool your feet in the little stream.

As you continue around the circuit you can marvel at the fact that this stunning beauty spot is actually manmade. The area's Victorian owners decided that, while the wild, tree-covered moorland was undeniably breathtaking, it could be better; so they set about damming the beck that drained the dell to create the tarns you see today. The Hows are the surrounding small, wooded hills.

This is also a good winter walk – its undulating but very easy-going trail will be trundle-able in all but the heftiest snowfalls, and the ice on the water and the frost on the trees add a new, jewelled splendour to the landscape.

OS map
Explorer OL7

how far
1⅕ miles

how long
1–1½ hours

how easy

Suitable for all buggies; there are no steep gradients.

a literary inspiration

When the tarn and its setting were put up for sale in 1929, they were bought by Beatrix Potter, who then sold the half containing Tarn Hows to the National Trust, and later bequeathed the rest of the estate to the Trust in her will. This amounted to more than 4,000 acres of land, including cottages and 15 farms. The legacy has helped to ensure that the Lake District and the practice of fell farming remain unspoiled.

dad fact!

The Norsemen who settled here in the 7th century referred to the area's small mountain lakes as 'tjorn', meaning teardrop. This poetic image is still with us in the related English word 'tarn'. 'Hows' comes from their word for hills – 'haugr'.

route

- The walk is very straightforward: cross the road at the car park entrance and you will see the well-made track.
- Simply follow it down the hill to the left to make a clockwise circuit of the lake, or head right, past the flattish picnic spot, to do the anticlockwise circuit.

getting there

From the A593 at Coniston, take the B5285 towards Hawkshead. At Hawkshead Hill, 1 mile before Hawkshead itself, turn left on the minor road, following signs for Tarn Hows. Park at the National Trust car park, **OS grid ref. SD326996**. You can also catch the Cross Lakes Experience bus in summer (www.lakedistrict.gov.uk/crosslakes).

rest and refresh

There are loos in the National Trust car park; an ice cream van visits in summer.
There are also several cafés in Hawkshead.

further info

www.nationaltrust.org.uk

route map

Map labels:
A593 to Ambleside
Yew Tree Tarn
A593
A593 to Coniston
Tarn Hows
National Trust House
Start/Finish
Viewpoint
P
To B5285 and Coniston
To B5285
N
0 ¼ mile

grizedale forest

Musical logs, wooden sheep, award-winning art, waterfalls, campsite, meditation classes and a Christmas tree shop – it could only be Grizedale, Lakeland's forest fantasyland.

Grizedale is the forest of fun. It's home to miles of thrilling mountain bike trails, an adventure playground and two motor rallies every year, but is so big (8,000 acres) that the adrenaline fans can zoom off and do their own thing and still leave plenty of peace for those of us who prefer a quiet wander through the woods.

There are plenty of walks, but rather than rush around trying to do everything on your first visit, we recommend you take your time (and a picnic) and simply savour this little 'starter for ten' saunter through the trees.

The route wanders in a figure-of-eight from the visitor centre, with a wooden bridge over a tumbling river gully. The path is suitable for all buggies (wheelchairs too) so you can just follow the wooden posts and lose yourself in the glories of the groves without mislaying any loved ones.

Just a few metres away from the visitor centre a field of wild flowers drops away to your right, opening up a splendid welcoming vista of the forest. Soon you'll be rolling through the trees – and what trees! The Forestry Commission has devoted years to restoring the oak, larch, spruce and pine woodland. Time and effort well spent.

Come here around dawn or dusk and you might see the last naturally afforested herd of red deer in England. Roe deer also roam free, while barn owls, buzzards and woodpeckers make their homes in the treetops. You can now glimpse red kites swooping over the woodland canopy, thanks to a successful reintroduction scheme, and rare white-faced darter dragonflies have been spotted hovering above the forest tarns.

Manmade wonders thrive here too, in the shape of 20 sculptures sited along the walk. Some of these can be played, hidden inside or scrambled over; just the sort of art that older children love. And if you don't spot them all – well, you'll be back here for more fun soon...

OS map
Explorer OL7

how far
1¼ miles

how long
1 hour

how easy

Very easy going; suitable for all buggies.

sculpture club

Grizedale's name comes from the Norse for 'valley of the wild boar'. There may be no boars in the woods now, but there are around 90 sculptures, many of which are made from natural materials such as stone and wood. Famous sculptors whose works have appeared here include David Nash, Sally Matthews and Andy Goldsworthy.

dad fact!

In World War II the only people who would have been enjoying these woods were German officers – the nearby Grizedale Hall was used as a prisoner of war camp. They must have enjoyed the space – most of the prisoners were taken from sunken U-boats and the Hall was nicknamed the 'U-boat Hotel'. Unfortunately, this stately home was demolished in 1957.

route

- From the car park, turn right in front of the loos and go past the striking Yan building, then simply follow the blue waymarked posts for the Ridding Wood Walk.
- Where the route zigzags back on itself you can continue on a little further, to a bench at a viewpoint, before returning.

getting there

Grizedale Forest is 3 miles south-west of Hawkshead, on the road to Satterthwaite, and is clearly signposted. The car park is at **OS grid ref. SD336943**. The Cross Lakes Shuttle bus service, which runs between Windermere and Ambleside, stops here during the summer (www.lakedistrict.gov.uk/crosslakes).

rest and refresh
The Grizedale visitor centre has a children's playground, education centre, café, loos and a shop.

further info
Visitor centre: 01229 860010; www.forestry.gov.uk

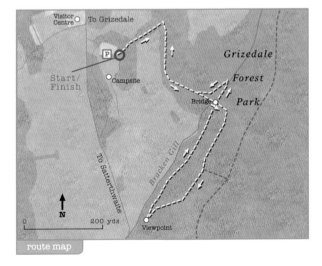

route map

aysgarth falls

Feel the force of tumbling water at a solid mile of beautiful waterfalls, then amble your way through the surrounding woods and farmland for glorious views of Wensleydale.

Waterfalls are like fires – stare at them for just a few moments and suddenly you can become utterly lost. Your eyes are danced to distraction by the endless pattern of movement while the constant, complex music drowns out the world around you and stills your thoughts.

Aysgarth Falls aren't particularly tall or wide, but they have a powerful drama that's all their own. The River Ure surges over sheer limestone lips and plummets into boiling pools, gathering its strength for half a second before galloping headlong over the next drop. It's easy to see why Turner came here in 1816 to capture this beauty on canvas. Wordsworth brought his notebook and was also flooded with creative inspiration.

There are three Falls: Upper, Middle and Lower, which drop 30 metres in total. They're named after their position on the river rather than their size: the Lower Falls are the tallest. Thousands of years ago, vast glaciers ground out the valley, revealing sandwiched layers of hard limestone and soft shale. Water then ate out the shale, cutting free blocks of limestone and creating the angular drops. Today they display a snapshot of the centuries of constant surging violence that brought them into being.

You could just follow the trails to the Falls and return to the café for a cuppa, but we prefer to loop lazily through some drowsy woods to a lesser-known corner of the valley. Cool tunnels under arching branches offer a soothing contrast to the crashing cataracts, and the scene opens out over farmland to unveil wider views of Wensleydale. And if you go in spring, the woodland floor will be a blooming sea of bright wild flowers.

There is a rather idiosyncratic diversion, where a farmer insists you zigzag through his field rather than walking a further 100 metres along the track you are already on. But it's short and gives you a fine chance to admire Castle Bolton in the distance – plus the sheep don't seem to mind.

OS map
Explorer OL30

how far
2⅖ miles

how long
2–2½ hours

how easy

Mostly good paths and grass/ farm tracks; some knobbly bits; optional steps.

take care

Being a no-nonsense sort of county, Yorkshire only nods to Health and Safety, and you can get very close to the Lower Falls – in fact, you could easily step into them. This makes it handy to pose for a very scenic picture, but if you do decide to take the buggy down from the main path, please be very careful.

dad fact!

Aysgarth Falls lent their drama to the 1991 Kevin Costner film *Robin Hood: Prince of Thieves*. Robin fought Little John at the Upper Falls and got a ducking for his troubles.

route

- From the car park, follow signs for the Middle and Lower Falls, crossing the road and heading into the wood.
- Take the short detour down to the Middle Falls – best leave the buggy at the top of the steps – then return to the path and continue to the turning for the Lower Falls.
- Either leave the buggy here and go down and back to the Lower Falls or you can take the buggy down on the little loop that visits the viewing rocks, but do be careful.
- Return to the path and follow the signs for Castle Bolton.
- The path rises across a field and passes a farm. Follow the detour across a field and back to the farm track.
- Turn left, back towards Aysgarth, on the footpath beside a dismantled railway.
- Head through a field, past the lone oak tree, and go left under an old railway bridge.
- Turn immediately right and weave through the wood until you reach the car park.
- Pass right through and follow the signed route to Upper Falls, afterwards returning on this same path.

getting there

Aysgarth is on the A684 between Hawes and Leyburn. The National Park Centre is just north of the village, and is signed from the main road. Take the turning, cross the river, then turn left just before the railway bridge to park at the National Park Centre itself, **OS grid ref. SE012887**.

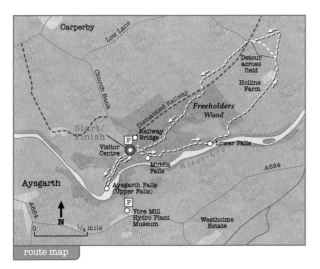

route map

rest and refresh

There is a café by the car park at the National Park Centre, as well as public loos.
The Falls café/bar in Aysgarth village has spacious facilities.

further info

www.yorkshiredales.org.uk

grass woods

Lose yourself in ancient woodland before picnicking in a water meadow by the snoozy River Wharfe on this gem of a walk, which even ambles past a favourite Dales town too.

Grassington is about as bustling as you want a place to be when you're winding down in the dales. Wander its tiny streets to take your pick of charming and arty shops, and it's easy to find a cosy café or lay your outstretched fingers on some ridiculously tasty ice cream.

You'll probably also notice that the locals seem addicted to getting together and having a laugh. In the last two weeks of June, the town hosts Grassington Festival, showcasing an eclectic mix of music, film, drama, comedy, walks and even an Art Trail. The town sponsors its own Victorian theatre company, which you can regularly see performing on the streets; there's a monthly farmers' market; and a Dickensian Festival in December. When do they just stay home and watch telly? Not often, it seems.

Come during the summer festival and you're likely to see the town's little cobbled square filled with a sun-kissed crowd jumping to the beats of a drum-and-kazoo troupe. And once you've had your fill of that sort of thing, this walk, in nearby Grass Woods, offers a cool and quiet interlude. Here you'll meet just a handful of people, and the only music will be the trilling of songbirds.

The route is a plain circle through the woods but, if you take your time, you'll make some surprising discoveries. This is the deepest pocket of broadleaved woodland remaining in the Yorkshire Dales and it attracts dozens of bird species to hold their own Grassington Festival here. With luck and patience you'll spot treecreepers; nuthatches; blue, coal and marsh tits; woodcocks; warblers and great spotted woodpeckers singing and showing off in the trees.

Just across the leafy lane from where you park, a rough path down through more woods suddenly brings you out into a grassy meadow sweeping round a lazy bend of the River Wharfe. It's the perfect picnic spot and a fine finale that turns this circular walk into a 'Q'. For Quiet.

OS map
Explorer OL2

how far
3⅕ miles

how long
2–2½ hours

how easy

Mostly good going with a few steep sections and some narrow paths. You'll need to carry the buggy during the descent to the water meadow.

long-term love affair

A notice pinned by the side of the path explains the plans of the woods' owners, the Wildlife Trust: they are returning the forest to its full native glory by growing out the alien conifers planted by misguided former landlords. And you can't help but be impressed by their dedication; they aim to have the woods looking their mature best in about 200 years from now.

dad fact!

In the woods is the site of a fort built to repel Roman invaders by the Brigantes, the Celtic tribe who once controlled much of Yorkshire. You can also see the foundations of an Iron Age settlement.

route

- Turn left out of the car park and walk back along the road a little, to a gate into the woods on your left.
- Go through the gate and follow the path up, then take the next left, so that the fence is on your right.
- Continue on until the path drops into a clearing near the road. There's an information board here. Take the wide forest track uphill.
- After the path bends right it goes over a crossroads, then a grassy track heads to the right.
- You can add in a little loop to the Iron Age settlement here by going straight on and returning over the 'scar', or hill.
- After the right turn, the path rises slightly then starts its final descent.
- Go over a crossroads, follow the path to the right, take the next left then next right. When you see the road, turn right and follow the wall back to the start.
- The path to the river starts on the opposite side of the road and is best tackled with two people. Simply tootle along the riverside for as long as you like, returning the same way.

getting there

The walk starts 1 mile north-west of Grassington, in Wharfedale, on the minor road to Conistone. This can be reached from the A59 between Skipton and Harrogate. Take the B6160 north near Bolton Bridge and at Threshfield turn right, crossing the river and turning left when you reach Grassington. Park at the old quarry, **OS grid ref. SD985652**; there's also some roadside parking.

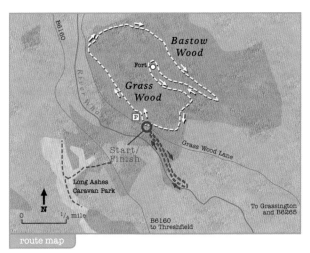

route map

rest and refresh

There are no facilities on the route itself, but there are loads of eateries to choose from in Grassington.

further info

www.grassington.uk.com
www.grassington-festival.org.uk

north east

brimham rocks

One minute you're striding across open moorland under big skies, the next you're twisting amid weird rock formations as your imagination tangles in knots of wonder.

It might seem odd that you can reach some of the UK's most sensational rock formations, perched high on a Yorkshire hilltop, by buggy – but you can.

Brimham Rocks is an amazing group of bizarre, and often gravity-defying, naturally sculpted stones. Some have to be seen to be believed – Idol Rock is a massive 200-ton stone that balances on a tiny narrow plinth. Others are also famous enough to have their own name – the Dancing Bear, the Druid's Writing Desk, the Camel, the Flowerpot – but there are dozens of other curious formations, just waiting to be titled by creative young minds. (Fans of children's TV show *Roger and the Rottentrolls* will recognise many shapes – the show was filmed here.)

The rocks are located on top of one of the best viewpoints in the county. The glorious panoramas open up at several points on the walk, particularly near the Druid's Writing Desk (or Wonky Mushroom, as we termed it), where there are spectacular vistas over Nidderdale and beyond.

There's a simple looping path through the site and you could scoot round in an hour or so. But you'll have far more fun if you just lose yourself in the labyrinth of by-paths that creep around tottering towers and lead under wind-worn arches. There are 50 acres of stones, so let your imagination run riot – at times it'll feel like you're an extra wandering through the set of a surrealist movie.

You can also explore some of the paths that roll over the surrounding moorland – it's easy to pick up one of the tracks that head west into the valley. Soon you'll be out on your own amid the heather, with a view behind you of the rocks crowning the hilltop.

Why not pack a picnic and follow your nose through the crazy pinnacles until you find a nice table-like rock to lay your sandwiches on? Then simply sit down, stretch out and feast on a banquet of food, fresh air and fun.

OS map
Explorer 298

how far
1¹⁄₁₀ miles for the basic loop, many extra paths through the rocks too.

how long
1 hour for the loop; more if you explore the other paths.

how easy

The loop path is generally wide and firm under-wheel; narrower grass tracks to reach some stones.

climb and clamber

If you have any older children you'll see them for about 10 seconds of this walk, before they disappear over a boulder. And why not? Although it's a National Trust site, this isn't a stately home where 'Do Not Touch' rules the roost. These stones are to be enjoyed – they're even made of a particularly good rock type for climbing: Millstone Grit.

dad fact!

The rocks started life as sediment deposits at the bottom of a delta, around 320 million years ago. The shapes were then sculpted by ice ages. That's the scientific explanation. One more romantic possibility is that a Frost Giant carved the shapes as ornaments for his back garden. Your turn.

route

- Take the rising path to the left-hand side of the road that heads on from the car park.
- Follow the obvious pathway as it weaves through the many rock formations.
- When you reach the café, head to the left, up the angled road to the visitor centre.
- Before you reach this building, take the path to the left.
- Follow this round, past several more formations, until you pass the impossibly balanced Idol Rock.
- Just after this, bear right to head along the edge of the moorland of Brimham Moor.
- Keep this on your left as you work your way back through more formations to reach the car park again.

getting there

From the A61 at Ripon, take the B6265 heading for Pateley Bridge. After 8 miles, turn left onto the minor road that is signed for Brimham Rocks (not 'Brimham Rocks Cottages'). The National Trust car park is at **OS grid ref. SE208645**.

rest and refresh

The visitor centre has a café and loos. There is a lot of open space around this and plenty of picnic spots around the rocks. There's usually an ice cream van in the car park too.

further info

Visitor centre: 01423 780688; www.nationaltrust.org.uk

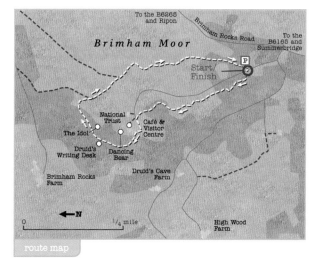

route map

nidderdale

Old stone farmhouses stand high on the hill; the river twists its way through hayfields; craggy moors rise into view above the trees. A northern Eden is laid out before you...

As you drive past Nidderdale's ivy-clad pubs, rolling fields and riverside picnic spots, you may wonder why you have to keep going. But when you start this walk, by trip-trapping over a stone bridge and sauntering beside the sun-freckled stream overhung with sleepy trees, you'll know it was worth the extra mile or two.

This little tour of Upper Nidderdale shows you all the beauties of a Yorkshire Dale in miniature, without any of the crowds or caravans. Muscled hills cradle a twisting river in a deep embrace, lush farmland clothing their lower slopes while their moorland tops are bare to the skies. Nidderdale is perhaps the least well-known of the Dales, and it feels more like a working landscape than a tourist destination. You probably won't meet anyone else on this intimate walk; unless you count sheep, cows and chickens, in which case it might feel like rush hour.

After the initial riverside ramble, there's a stiff push up a zigzagging stony track, but the brief burst of puffing is definitely worth it. That's the hard work of the walk smartly done and now you can savour the views.

Splashing through a fun little ford, you'll enjoy the lofty lookout of a farm road that runs at a constant height around the elbow of the dale. A gaggle of farmhouses perches here like birds on a wire, surveying the valley floor proprietorially. Solitary ancient oaks give way to shady stands of pine as the route rounds the elbow of the crooked dale. Here you can see west up the valley to the high dam of Scar House Reservoir and south towards the snuggled hamlet of Lofthouse.

The path trundles cheekily through someone's front garden before it winds back down to earth on a bracken-covered hillside. The last bit of fun is crossing a dry riverbed; it's only a few metres wide and easy with two people. There's just time for a doe-eyed farewell from the resident cows before you return to the quiet valley road.

OS map
Explorer 298

how far
3⅖ miles

how long
2½–3 hours

how easy

Mostly good tracks, but there can be some mud – wellies advisable in winter. A hard (but short) climb and a brief portage across a dry river.

stealing the scene

Nidderdale's glorious moorland scenery and tapestry of lush, green meadows have rightfully earned its status as an area of outstanding natural beauty. It is bordered by the Yorkshire Dales National Park and is close to Fountains Abbey. Its charms have attracted generations of artists, photographers and film-makers; it had a starring role in the 1970 film of *Wuthering Heights*.

dad fact!

If you fancy adding some adrenaline to your day, visit How Stean Gorge (www.howstean.co.uk) near Lofthouse. This spectacular limestone chasm is more than half a mile in length and up to 20 metres deep. You can explore caves, tunnels and one of only two *via ferratas* in England.

route

- From the parking spot, follow the road up Nidderdale for 600 metres until you see a track going down to your right.
- Take this, cross the river then turn left, following a farm track parallel to the water.
- After ¼ mile, the path heads up the slope to the right, past a barn.
- There's a steep zigzagging section, then a tiny stream crosses the path and the route now heads back east on a high-level track.
- Pass several farmhouses, then follow the track around the corner of the valley.
- Just after passing through the grounds of Thwaite House, the path drops steeply down to the valley floor and across a dry riverbed.
- Follow the signs through the farmyard back to the road, turn right and return to your car.

getting there

Nidderdale is accessed on a minor road running north from the B6265 at Pateley Bridge. Continue, through Ramsgill, towards Middlesmoor. Just past Lofthouse the road crosses the River Nidd, then there's a track on the right that leads to Scar House Reservoir; follow this north for 2 miles. Just before it bends west, take the old railway tunnel entrance on the left and park here: **OS grid ref. SE099765**.

rest and refresh

There are no facilities on the route, but there are several welcoming pubs in Nidderdale.
The Crown Hotel at Lofthouse is friendly and has outdoor space.
There are also several family-friendly cafés in Pateley Bridge, including Just Delicious (01423 711595; www.just-delicious.co.uk).

further info

www.nidderdale.co.uk
www.visitnidderdaleaonb.com

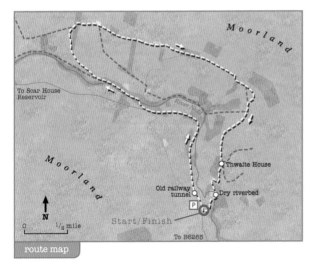

route map

jervaulx abbey

Visit the ruins of Jervaulx Abbey and you'll enjoy a place of pure spiritual calm, where wild flowers twist round ruined pillars and grass carpets the nave of a once lofty chapel.

Peace. That's the first feeling that the tumbledown stones of Jervaulx instil as you wander around them. However long the medieval monks worked to build their mighty abbey and sustain their lands, it is also clear that this was a place of true spiritual power for them.

Their buildings may now be in ruins, but the tranquillity they discovered here has endured for you to discover today. Dark corners once lit with shining candles are now splashed with the light of 180 species of wild flowers. Majestic yew trees line ancient cloisters and, where once the sombre incantations of psalms rose to the rafters, now the music of birds rings to the blue vault above.

Jervaulx Abbey was founded in 1156 by Cistercian monks who left Byland Abbey in the nearby moors in search of a less bleak location. They were granted land in Wensleydale, the fertile valley of the River Ure. For four centuries the holy men developed their new home, building a beautiful church and expanding its lands to at one point cover half of the valley. In 1537 the monastery was dissolved by Henry VIII and it has lain in ruins ever since.

Today it is in private hands and exploring its grassy nooks makes for a very relaxing little amble. The entry fee is by honesty box; a warm and trusting welcome to the walk. From there you can simply wander where you will, and let your imagination fly back through history. You'll soon form a picture of the abbey's former glory.

Every little doorway and hidden window reveals a new surprise: a water trough, an ancient kitchen, a row of elegant arches or a pheasant sunning itself on a bench.

Once you've supped your fill of serenity (and finished your picnic) at the abbey you can take a little stroll through the surrounding rolling parkland, where sheep drift over gentle hills and swans paddle on a sheltered pond. It's easy to imagine living out a lifetime of quiet days here.

OS map
Explorer 302

how far
2⅖ miles

how long
2 hours

how easy

Good track, grassy path and road; the track is slightly stony in places.

ale and arty

The nearby town of Masham is well worth exploring. It's home to one of the UK's oldest markets (chartered in 1250) and boasts the brilliant Theakston and Black Sheep breweries. It also has a famous Sheep Fair in September and an Arts Festival every two years.

dad fact!

Jervaulx's founding monks were originally from the Roquefort region of France, and it was they who created Wensleydale cheese, initially made from sheep's milk. Wensleydale is most notable, of course, for being the favourite cheese of Wallace from the *Wallace and Gromit* films.

route

- Cross the road from the car park and pass through the gate.
- Go straight on where the path crosses a bridleway, heading towards the abbey.
- Pay at the honesty box and go in.
- After exploring the abbey's gentle spaces, return to the path junction and turn left.
- Walk through the parkland, past the pond, to a gatehouse.
- Here you can simply stop and retrace your steps, or turn right, onto the road for a few hundred metres before following the sign back into the park on your right to make a little loop.

getting there

Jervaulx Abbey is 5 miles north-east of Masham, on the A6108. The car park is signposted, and is at **OS grid ref. SE168856**.

rest and refresh

There is a tea room with loos by the car park; several cafés and family-friendly pubs in nearby Masham.

Also worth a visit is nearby High Jervaulx Farm, which makes its own delicious ice cream (01677 460337; www.abmoore.co.uk).

The parlour boasts over 35 flavours as well as ice cream gateaus...

further info

www.jervaulxabbey.com

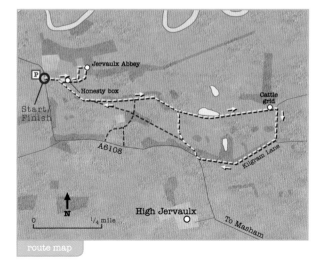

route map

sutton bank

Rarely do the most stupendous views and simplest paths come so neatly together as at Sutton Bank. Yorkshire spreads out at your feet as you follow this high escarpment trail.

Sutton Bank is steep. Caravans are banned and HGVs should know better, but still they get stuck on the winding road that tracks up this sheer edge of Yorkshire moor. The benefit of all this gravity is a spellbinding view over the quilted Vale of York, which unrolls itself all the way to the dales on the far side. And although the location may be precipitous, two simple walks spread out along the escarpment edge like soaring wings. If you're feeling really energetic, you can combine them in a large loop.

The first walk takes you to the head of the White Horse of Kilburn, which is cut into the steep limestone bank and visible for miles around. As in the case of a real nag, the most majestic view of the horse itself isn't to be had from the top of its ears. It does, however give you a fascinating peek into its construction. Unlike the hillsides of south England, here there's no layer of chalk lurking just beneath the topsoil. This horse is made of grey limestone pebbles that have to be regularly whitewashed to maintain the design. The noble steed was originally dug into the hillside by children from the local school. Today they'd get community service for such a stunt, but in 1857 the locals were impressed by their 67-metre high hillside graffiti, and even helped finish it off.

The flat acres you pass on your left might seem like fields, but they are actually the runway of the local gliding club. If conditions are right, you'll see these elegant aviators wheeling effortlessly on the thermals above you. Stay a little and you can also watch them take off and land – but keep your head down!

The other wing of the walk flies out to the north west, above Lake Gormire. This liquid emerald is set in a circlet of ancient woodland and is one of only three natural lakes in Yorkshire. As you sit on a bench and gaze out from this airy eyrie, it's easy to agree with author James Herriot, who lived just a few miles from here, and believed this view was 'the finest in England'.

OS map
Explorer OL26

how far
route a: 3¹⁄₁₀ miles; **route b:** 2 miles; **route c:** 5½ miles

how long
route a: 2 hours; **route b:** 1½ hours; **route c:** 3½–4½ hours

how easy
all routes

Paths are mostly suitable for all abilities, as well as wheelchairs; **route c** has some stretches on grassier and bumpier country lanes.

ice sculpture
The Vale of York was a vast river of ice 20,000 years ago. This scraped along the western edge of the moors, gouging out the soft underlying rocks to create the escarpment. As the climate warmed, meltwater cut further channels at the base of the cliff. In some places, mud deposits and landslides blocked up these channels, forming small lakes like Gormire, which is fed by underground drainage and produces springs nearby.

dad fact!
Below Sutton Bank is the village of Sutton-under-Whitestonecliffe, which has the longest name of any place in England, at 27 letters.

route a

- From the visitor centre, cross the A170 and follow the signs for Walk 1 – The White Horse Walk – along the escarpment.
- When Walk 1 deviates to the right, ignore this and just continue to the top of the horse. Return the way you came.

route b

- From the centre, follow 'Walk 2' along Sutton Brow, ignoring the path downhill to the left after 400 metres, to continue along the cliff-top track, past the flat gallops on your right.
- Pass the end of Lake Gormire, below, and continue past a bridleway on your right. Carry on to the viewpoint on an outcrop. Turn here and follow your steps back to the start.

route c

- From the centre, follow Walk 1 signs to the white horse.
- Ignore the steps that drop down the hill; follow the path to the left that heads away from the cliff before joining the minor road that passes the gliding club; when it reaches the A170, cross over and turn right, into Hambleton.
- Turn left on a track that heads past Hambleton House. After ⅛ mile this joins a road for 200 metres, then take the bridleway that goes left at Dialstone Farm for about a mile.
- At the cliff edge, go left to follow the Sutton Brow path back.

getting there

Pass through Sutton-under-Whitestonecliffe and ascend the steep zigzags of Sutton Bank. The North York Moors National Park visitor centre is at the top, on the left, **OS grid ref. SE515830**.

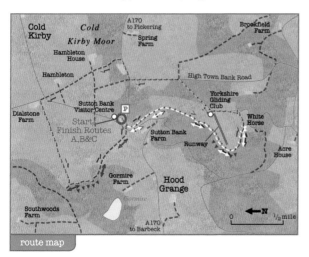

route map

rest and refresh

The tea room at the visitor centre is particularly fine, offering really hearty meals at reasonable prices. The centre also has an exhibition, information desk, countryside bookshop and accessible loo.

further info

Visitor centre: 01845 597426; www.northyorkmoors.org.uk
This walk also gets a huge thumbs-up for being very accessible by public transport. The Moors Bus stops regularly at the visitor centre daily in August and September, and on Sundays and Bank Holidays from April to October.

esk valley

Young hands wave in glee at the steam train chuffing past, out of the trees, and all aboard wave back. Their joy is so infectious even non-train-fans will love this walk back in time.

The moor stretches in every direction like a heather-clad prairie. Then the road begins to fall, slowly at first and then steeply, like a rollercoaster. And suddenly the bleak heights are behind you and a sheltered valley with toytown charms is spread out below; cottages snoozing on the hillside, green fields neatly diced by stone walls, a lazy river and a perfectly restored steam railway.

There's something about the puffing of steam that gets everyone excited. And in Grosmont the whole town is steam-doolally – this is where the main rail network meets the North Yorkshire Moors Railway, Britain's favourite heritage line. The station sits at the heart of the village, and it pumps a magical energy through its streets – no wonder it was Hogwarts station in the *Harry Potter* films.

Our wizardly adventure starts with a ride on one of the lovingly restored trains. Pop your buggy in the guard's van and climb aboard a wood-panelled carriage. As you wheesh through the tunnel and out into the fields you'll soon be under the old railway's spell. Alighting at Goathland, you'll wish the journey had been longer – until you spy the station tea room. The service is from a golden age; the tables built into old coal wagons. One lump or two?

All this fun and you still have the delights of the walk ahead of you. Now it's time to return along the track bed of an even older railway that runs parallel to the line you just travelled on. You'll see more trains puffing out of the trees as you meander past sheep-speckled fields.

Halfway through the walk, a leafy lane leads to the one-street hamlet of Beck Hole, where the Birch Hall Inn is a must-stop. Is there another pub in the world with its own sweetshop sandwiched between the bar and the saloon? Time seems to stand still here; it's easy to idle away a sun-dappled hour or so in the leafy riverside beer garden. From there it's a simple cruise through the Esk Valley's deep green groove back to the bewitching streets of Grosmont.

OS map
Explorer OL27

how far
3⁷⁄₁₀ miles

how long
20 minutes on the train;
2–3 hours walking

how easy

The track is easy going and downhill for most of the route; a handful of steps at the very end.

making tracks

The North Yorkshire Moors Railway was closed in 1965, but local residents loved it so much that they had it up and running again within eight years. The steam trains, stations, cafés and workshops are all manned by volunteers. This is their hobby, so you'll find the conductors, drivers and tea room staff almost invariably smiling. If this creates an idealised railway, well, that's all just part of its charm.

dad fact!

One of the engineers who designed the line got carried away and put an ornate castle-like entrance on one of the tunnels. The owner was furious at him for wasting money. But it's lovely, and today you can walk through the tunnel to visit the engine sheds.

5MT

45407

route

- Board the train at Grosmont, sitting in one of the last three carriages. (Buy your ticket on the train – it was £5 per adult when we went, and under-5s go free!)
- Get out at the first stop, Goathland. Head out of the station up the steep access road.
- After passing a pub, turn right and cross the car park to a wooden gate.
- This path goes steeply downhill before settling into a gentler gradient.
- After a mile and a bit, you can turn right to visit Beck Hole.
- Turn right when you reach the road and cross the bridge to get to the sweetie-selling pub.
- Rejoin the path and continue down the valley, crossing the river and passing through quiet fields.
- Near Grosmont comes the only tricky bit, a steep climb with a few steps to go over the hill that the trains go under.
- Drop down past a church and you pop out at the station.

getting there

From the A169 between Pickering and Whitby, take the minor road signposted 'Grosmont' (pronounced 'grow-mont') about 5 miles south of Whitby. Park in the pay and display area beside the station, **OS grid ref. NZ827053**. This is a busy little village, so it's worth thinking about using public transport to get here.

rest and refresh

You'll find refreshments at Grosmont, Goathland and the Birch Hall Inn at Beck Hole (www.beckhole.info/bhi.htm)

There are loos at Grosmont and Goathland.

further info

The North Yorkshire Moors Railway: www.nymr.co.uk

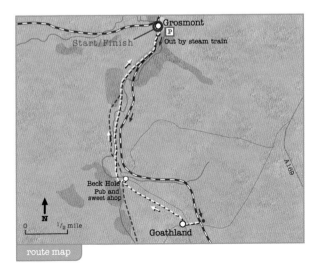

route map

allen banks

Insects dance over shining water and banks of flowers perfume the air. Meander with the river through a gorge so lush and leafy even weary adults will look for elves at play here.

This is the perfect walk to do when other routes in the great wild north are too blowy or a little damp. The gusts won't disturb you in the gorge, and is there anything more relaxing than the pat-and-flap of rain on oak leaves? Put the cover on the buggy, bring your brolly and enjoy a drizzly day to remember.

At Allen Banks you roll upstream through a treelined river valley, inhaling nature's purest airs. Then you return, enjoying the beauty from another viewpoint as the stream chatters irrepressibly beside you, a liquid ticker tape taking its news from the mountains to the sea.

Once you've left the car park and joined the sinuous but easy-going path that nestles under trees' fringes, you'll get your first glimpse of what this walk is all about: clear water, brown stones, wild flowers and green tree tunnels.

This ravishing ravine doesn't change much along its length, but that's part of its charm. It's so simple that you can switch your brain off, stop looking for things and let them come to you. If you're quiet enough you'll realise that the particularly rapid splash you just heard wasn't water on rock, but fish belly on water. It might become apparent that you can smell more varieties of flower than you can see. And that very *Indiana Jones*y bridge which, ordinarily, would look far too tricky for a buggy might today make for a rather fun family photo.

After three-quarters of a mile the river bends sharply to the right. This is a good place to turn around as the way becomes rockier and rootier, so only push on if you're feeling particularly adventurous. You can also get down to the river fairly easily here to skim stones and paddle.

You could also pause on any of the several log benches en route and let the busy river carry a few cares away. Many of these benches have plaques with poems on, just in case you weren't feeling contemplative enough.

OS map
Explorer OL43

how far
1⅗ miles

how long
1–2 hours

how easy

The going is generally smooth, but there are some rooty sections and if you take the optional loop back there are a few steps.

all along the watchtower

On a crag above the gorge stand the ruins of a medieval watchtower, Staward Peel. Peel towers were built along the England/Scotland border as a kind of early warning system of invasion. Each required an iron basket at its summit, fuelled and ready to be quickly lit to warn of approaching danger.

dad fact!

The walk used to be part of the pleasure grounds of nearby Ridley Hall. The car park is in the estate's old walled garden. This was ingeniously designed with fireplaces and flues in its walls to extend the growing seasons of fruit and vegetables. The walk is now part of the largest area of ancient woodland in the North Pennines AONB.

route

- From the car park, walk past the picnic tables and enter the wood.
- The path is clear and follows the river closely.
- Turn around where the river kinks west at **OS grid ref. NY798629** and head back the way you came.
- Returning, you can add a loop by heading up the ramp to your left.
- This will open up views of Ridley Hall and the hills beyond, but you will have to carry the buggy down around 20 steps near the end. It's worth it if there are two of you.

getting there

The walk is signposted from the A69 just west of Haydon Bridge. Leave your car at the National Trust car park (pay and display), **OS grid ref. NY798641**.

rest and refresh

There are loos and picnic tables by the car park.

further info

National Trust: 01434 344218; www.nationaltrust.org.uk

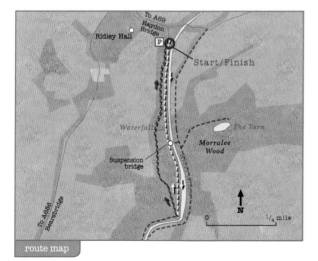

route map

kielder water

You might feel that a spray-splashed spin on *The Osprey* ferry is adventure enough, but your woodland return offers red squirrels, roe deer and otters to thrill keen young eyes.

As *The Osprey* ferry skims you over white-crested waves and you roll out onto the wooden jetty, you may be forgiven for feeling a little lost. There are no houses on the hills ringing the horizon. No major roads come this way. Deer wander freely and there are more barn owls in the trees around you than there are people in this spot. Welcome to the largest manmade forest in Europe and the shining gem at its heart – Kielder Water.

On the map the lake looks like a wild winged serpent, wriggling its way through the northern hills. But this potentially tricky beast has been tamed by a trail that encircles the whole lake in a 27-mile-long lasso. There are many places where you can just pull up and enjoy a wander, but the peninsula of Bull Crag offers a satisfying loop or an exciting one-way trip with a ferry ride.

The path weaves in and out of narrow inlets where otters go hunting. The moorland is alive with birds, and even the working forest is beautiful in its way. Every twig of every harvested tree is put to good use: the trunk for timber, the top and limbs for fencing and the rest for cardboard. Fields of felled trees may seem desolate at first, but look closely and you'll see hidden treasures. As the stumps rot they give nutrients back to the soil and provide a haven for insects, small reptiles and mammals. Each becomes a sylvan skyscraper for societies of tiny creatures.

The woods are not just pines; you will wander through stands of majestic beech trees that remember when all around were fields. Red squirrels have wisely made this one of their last English hideouts, and you can wait for them to start bickering over beechnuts from a special hide.

As you point out all this beauty to your little one, it's hard to believe that this whole landscape only came into being when the North Tyne was dammed in the 1970s. Still, as manmade feats go, Kielder beats the shopping centre for wandering on a blue-skied Sunday in spring – paws down.

OS map
Explorer OL42

how far
route a: 5⅞ miles
route b: 4⅞ miles

how long
route a: 4–5 hours
route b: 30 minutes on ferry;
3–4 hours walking

how easy
both routes

The path is mostly excellent, with a few stony sections, a softer section in the woods and a stretch on a disused tarmac road.

return of the native

Ospreys are once again nesting in Northumberland after a 200-year absence. You can view these magnificent and endangered birds in their nests from two miles away through high-powered telescopes at Leaplish Waterside Park.

dad fact!

The park has been installing beautiful art and architecture for over 15 years. There are more than 20 pieces to see within 16 square miles of forest, making this the largest outdoor public art gallery in the UK.

route a

- From the car park, take the marked waterside path through the trees.
- Pass along an avenue of beeches to a fishermen's hut.
- The path follows the shoreline out onto the Bull Crag Peninsula, becoming a metalled road near the point.
- If you're feeling tired here, head back the way you came. But if you're full of beans and, more importantly, still have lots of snacks, then push on and make a loop out of it.
- The road becomes a trail again, which you follow round to a car park and picnic site.
- Take the road until you see a sign directing you to the right for Leaplish over the neck of the headland.
- You'll soon be back on the path through the beeches.

route b

- *The Osprey* ferry welcomes pushchairs. Take it from Leaplish Waterside Park to the Tower Knowe visitor centre and walk back along the clearly signposted waterside path.
- Note: It's wise to book the ferry at busy times.

getting there

From the A68, take the minor road to Bellingham. At Bellingham, turn left onto the B6320 and follow this road as it turns left over the river, then after 400 metres turn right onto the unclassified road heading west to Hesleyside and Kielder Water. Leaplish Waterside Park is well signposted from this road. Leave your car at the car park (pay and display) at **OS grid ref. NY660878**.

rest and refresh

Leaplish Waterside Park has a bar, shop, toilets, swimming pool, play park, birds of prey centre and the maddest crazy golf course we've ever seen. Wallabies, too.

further info

www.visitkielder.com

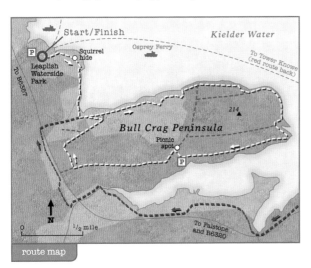

Route map: Start/Finish, Kielder Water, Osprey Ferry, To Tower Knowe (red route back), Squirrel hide, Leaplish Waterside Park, To B6357, Bull Crag Peninsula, 214, Picnic spot, P, N, ½ mile, To Falstone and B6320

route map

dunstanburgh castle

Ruined towers frown down at you from their cliff-top eyrie, boisterous waves are smashed into spray on the rocks and fresh sea air fills your lungs; this is a spirit-stirring coast tour.

Here's a walk that's something of a Cinderella character. Banished to a far-flung corner of Northumberland, where the North Sea pounds the rocky shore, this shy route has charms that outshine many a more famous beauty spot.

The approach through patchwork fields is pretty enough, but it does little to alert you to the varied pleasures of this nook of the north. It's only when you step out from the grass-backed dunes that you'll see how special this place is.

The walk hugs the rugged seashore then loops through rich farmland to form a ring that holds Dunstanburgh Castle fast in a rocky setting. Once the home of John of Gaunt, this snaggle-toothed cluster of brooding towers was already a ruin in 1538. But for nearly 500 years it has defied the pounding sprays and salt-laden winds of this exposed coast and clung to life on its lonely outcrop. Watch out for the kestrels, who love to hover here, scanning the long grasses for their lunch.

The National Trust owns the castle, and it's worth the charge for entry: wandering around these ruins is rather uplifting. It's as if contemplating all those medieval yesterdays suspends any fretting about impending tomorrows and leaves you happily becalmed in today.

But you'll still enjoy many stirring views if you decide to save your hard-earned pennies for a drink in the child-friendly Jolly Fisherman in Craster. From here the walk heads inland, across sweeping swards cropped lawn-short by sheep and amid fields that march towards distant hills. This more cultivated landscape has curios of its own: aged farm machinery, wartime pillboxes and brick furnaces.

This wander is so rich in treasures that the golden crescent of Embleton Bay, just 50 metres from where you parked, isn't even en route. If you still have any energy left you can explore its furrowed dunes and smooth sands before popping into Craster for that well-earned glass of milk.

OS map
Explorer 332

how far
3⅕ miles

how long
2–3 hours

how easy

Most of the walk is on good surfaces: paved road, wide track or smooth grass; the grass can be longer on the stretch by the golf course and the section just before the castle is rocky for 200 metres.

in the swim

The rocky cliff in front of the castle drops 46 metres into the sea. The waters at its base and around the nearby reefs are a favourite spot for divers, who come to explore the numerous wrecks and kelp forests. Keep an eye out also for the seals that often bask on the rocks.

dad fact!

Dunstanburgh is the largest castle in Northumberland, with an area of 11 acres. The massive stronghold was built by Earl Thomas of Lancaster, cousin of King Edward II. There are many other fine castles on this strategically important coast, including Bamburgh, which is almost as large as Dunstanburgh and is still inhabited.

route

- From the car park, head through the gate, then turn right and follow the access path along the edge of the golf course.
- The path cuts right in front of the 13th green, then there is a short rough section before you round the flank of the castle onto smooth grass.
- Head towards the sea, past the castle entrance, and follow the shore path towards a gate.
- After 50 metres, head inland, taking a path up and across the grass slope towards the skyline.
- Aim for the gap in the bush-covered mounds and follow the track up to some farm buildings.
- Turn right along a paved track through the fields.
- A little chicane through some farmhouses and a right turn will bring you back to the car.

getting there

From the A1, follow signs for Embleton. Take the road for Dunstan Steads, towards the beach, and park in the designated area, **OS grid ref. NU244224**.

rest and refresh
There are no facilities on the walk; Embleton and Craster have several good eateries and shops. The Jolly Fisherman pub (01665 576461) is famous for its homemade fresh crab soup.

further info
National Trust: 01665 576231; www.nationaltrust.org.uk www.visitnorthumberland.com

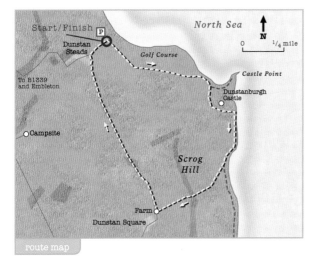

route map

index

Beautiful Buggy Walks: England
Researched, written and photographed by:
Richard Happer

Editor: Sophie Dawson
Design and cover: Harriet Yeomans
Proofreaders: Leanne Bryan, Catherine Greenwood,
Nikki Sims, Claire Wedderburn-Maxwell
Marketing: Shelley Bowdler
Publisher: Jonathan Knight

Published by: Punk Publishing, 3 The Yard, Pegasus
Place, London SE11 5SD

All photographs © Richard Happer except those on the
following pages (all reproduced with permission):
112–113, 137, 138–139 © Harriet Yeomans; 142
(bottom) © Abigail Yeomans.

Front cover: Muker, Swaledale, Yorkshire Dales,
England, UK © Peter J. Hatcher/Alamy

Route Maps © Mark Steward and Gordon MacGilp
(themapboy@yahoo.com).

Main Map p17 © MAPS IN MINUTES™/Collins
Bartholomew (2012).

Thanks to Mrs Carol Paxton for allowing us to use her
poem: 'Be Outside, Be Alive!' on p155.

The publishers and author have done their best to
ensure the accuracy of all information in *Beautiful
Buggy Walks: England*. However, they can accept no
responsibility for any injury, loss, or inconvenience
sustained by anyone as a result of information
contained in this book.

Punk Publishing takes its environmental
responsibilities seriously. This book has been printed
on paper made from renewable sources and we
continue to work with our printers to reduce our
overall environmental impact.

thanks to Emma, Andy, Belle and Leo
Summerscales; Margaret and Nigel Bullen; Jenny, Tim,
Will, Sam and George Humphries; Nick, Jo and Archie
Burgess; Helen, Raph, Lana and Lexi Miller; Emily,
Andy, Jasmine and Harris Greaves; Amanda and
Craig Burrow and family; Caroline, David, Conrad and
Magnus Phipps-Urch; Judith, Martin, Tom and Jamie
Fisher; Cal, Steve, Charlotte, Ellie and Alex Gisbourne;
Victor Slawski at the Langport & River Parrett visitor
centre; all at Abbotsbury Playgroup Group; Ray
Armstrong (and friend) for giving me a lift when
I blew a tyre in the middle of nowhere. And, of course,
Mark Happer and Ems Troke for cat-sitting beyond
the call of duty.

We hope you've enjoyed reading *Beautiful Buggy Walks:
England* and that it's inspired you to head out with your little
ones. The walks featured are a personal selection chosen by
the author. Richard Happer has roamed the country to find
this selection, but it hasn't been possible for him to visit every
single corner of Britain. So, if you know of a special buggy
walk that you think should be included in the next edition or
in *Beautiful Buggy Walks: Wales* and *Scotland*, please send an
email to hello@beautifulbuggywalks.co.uk telling us all about
it and why it's so special. We'll credit all useful contributions
in the next edition, and senders of the best emails will receive
a complimentary copy.